The
Rationed Years

The author in the uniform of
Senior Commander A.T.S.

THE
RATIONED YEARS

sequel to

Those Glittering Years

by

Alida Harvie

Regency Press (London & New York) Ltd.
125 High Holborn, London WC1V 6QA

ISBN 0 7212 0602 6

Printed and bound in Great Britain by
Buckland Press Ltd., Dover, Kent.

For my brother,
Group Captain R. E. G. Brittain, R.A.F. (Retd.),
who contributed his share, in four Continents,
towards the overthrow of the Nazi war machine.

Plate 1

Group Captain R. E. G. Brittain, R.A.F., my brother.

LIST OF ILLUSTRATIONS

Acknowledgements

Plates two, eight, ten, twelve and thirteen by kind permission of the Imperial War Museum.

AUTHOR'S NOTE

In my book *Those Glittering Years* I wrote a family story, touching the achievements of my late parents, Sir Harry and Dame Alida Brittain. I mentioned my father's founding of the Anglo-American Pilgrims' Society; his creation of the Imperial Press Conference, now the flourishing Commonwealth Press Union; his years in Fleet Street and Parliament; his many adventurous journeys and his connection with the British Travel Association, the Royal Overseas League, and the English-Speaking Union. Not least with his long contact with the U.S.A.

The book also referred to my mother's many musical accomplishments, her harp playing, and composition of harp music, and her life-long work with her husband in political and public affairs. In addition, I described my own childhood and adolescence in the between-the-wars era with many stories of a social life now completely vanished.

The Rationed Years is a sequel, dwelling largely on the thread of my personal experiences through the war-shattered 1940s, with a glimpse of the historical and social background of those stirring times.

CHAPTER ONE

The leaves were brown and golden in the autumn sunlight. It was now two months since Mr. Chamberlain's trembling voice had proclaimed that our country was at war with Germany on that vital September morning of 1939. Mr. Churchill was back in the Admiralty. An Expeditionary Force had crossed to France, Mussolini had announced his non-belligerence and President Roosevelt had established United States neutrality. The French Army had become invisible, securely hidden in the expensive depths of the Maginot Line.

A considerable proportion of the British Navy were centred in the Mediterranean, and the Poles, who had fought Hitler ferociously, and with the utmost bravery, overrun by Russia from the East, had now been conquered. Warsaw and other Polish towns were in ruins.

The sinking of merchant shipping was already heavy, the enemy using a completely untried weapon called "Magnetic Mines".

Now, three Baltic States, Latvia, Esthonia and Lithuania had been compelled by Russia to accept Russian military control. Finland's refusal, in a short and savage war, defiantly held the aggressor at bay until the spring, when a final agreement was reached.

There had been tragic news of the sinking of the aircraft carrier *Courageous* and the loss of the battleship *Royal Oak*.

The British Navy had, however, tracked down the German pocket battleship *Graf Spee* forcing her to take refuge at Montevideo. On Hilter's orders the *Graf Spee* was scuttled six miles outside the harbour. The German crew had been withdrawn, but the captain was thought to have committed suicide.

On the home front, now in the period of the "phoney war", many evacuated mothers and children, with battered cardboard boxes and dangling gas masks, had returned to their city homes.

Shining barrage balloons floated over London and other centres, piled sandbags protected doorways, windows were criss-crossed with brown tape against splintering glass, and some shops had been so securely protected that notices had had to be printed "We are open". The police wore steel helmets and carried lanterns.

At night the black-out was total. A few posters had appeared largely referring to National Savings: "*Your* resolution will bring *us* victory." One or two war songs had developed "Roll out the barrel" and "Hanging out the washing on the Siegfried Line". The latter was thought to have given some offence to the German forces.

A number of British citizens, in which actors and actresses were thought to be quite numerous, had left for America, causing the veteran actor Sir Seymour Hicks to write one of his characteristically witty letters to *The Times* "Gone with the wind up!"

Petrol had been rationed and the population had been issued with identity cards but food rationing was not to take place until 1940.

In our own personal world, life was progressing normally. We had moved from our London home, 2 Cowley Street, Westminster, and settled in our Hampshire cottage, Kirklands, which my mother had bought for the family for just such an eventuality in 1938. My R.A.F. brother, then squadron leader, who had found the cottage had persuaded us all to leave London. He himself had been posted to Fighter Command but his wife and two young children were accommodated in a farmhouse near Grantham. Thanks to the efforts of my sister-in-law, my father's lovely oak from Cowley Street had been sent to Grantham for safe keeping. My father and I had made any number of journeys by car rescuing smaller treasures but my mother's beautiful marquetry and many valuable pictures were still in place.

A staff of two had accompanied us to the cottage, our invaluable French cook, who had joined the family many years previously, and a young house-parlourman, as it was then called, who had only arrived a few months before the outbreak of war. This young man had a health defect which rendered him unfit for military service. Families like ours were approaching the "death-knell" of living-in domestic staff. "Dailies" or "Treasures" as they were to become called, would very soon supplant them. Meanwhile, we were remarkably lucky.

My mother's health at the beginning of the war was very frail. Asthma was a cruel affliction but this did not stop her from working hard at the Women's Institute meetings giving demonstrations of "Make do and Mend". She undertook a formidable amount of sewing herself.

My father, who had not resigned from business, travelled constantly to London on the Haslemere train.

My father's presence at home, and the availability of staff, was to enable me, the only daughter of the house, still in my twenties, to join the Women's Service known as F.A.N.Y. but not nearly as quickly as I would have liked. I had been transferred from the London Ambulance Unit, where I had trained, to Bordon, at my own request, and was now ensconced in a wooden hut with a telephone. Here I took turns with fellow ambulance drivers, mostly women, to remain on duty in four-hour shifts. We all used bicycles to save petrol, but at night it was considered wiser to travel by car. Driving at night was quite difficult, car headlamps were severely masked exposing small slits of light like candles spluttering in a wind. Cars had to be at once immobilised, when not in use, by removing the rota arm, and we were advised to paint the bodywork with white stripes or splashes and to tape the windows. On dark nights we were often grateful for the light of the searchlights energetically probing the black sky. Few air raid sirens had sounded up to that time, but the "banshee wail" as the newspapers called it, truly made one's blood run cold.

My father had secured a part-time gardener, but as this was now the epoch of "dig for victory" I did as much as I could to help when not on duty. My father, too, put in many valuable hours at week-ends in our vegetable plot.

As we approached December, military personnel were gathering at a considerable speed. In the Bordon area a huge contingent of Canadian forces had arrived. Army lorries rumbled along our local roads day and night.

First aid posts and air raid wardens were now numerous.

The Headley Village Hall had enterprisingly established a weekly cinema performance to keep up morale, and knitting was also underway. Many were the boring hours I was to spend knitting at the side of my ambulance unit telephone, making helmets in coarse khaki wool. Classes in first aid and home nursing were also starting.

At Christmas my brother had a few days leave bringing his family to Kirklands. My father's brother, who had emigrated to New Zealand in the 1920's, always known as Uncle Bob in the family circle, although his name was Bernard, sent the first of many generous food parcels which we were glad to share out with friends. My niece and nephew, then aged two-and-a-half years and eight months were to become another generation of war babies. Lord Woolton's skill as Food Minister was to serve them and all their young contemporaries extremely well.

It was a wonderfully happy family Christmas, the last we were ever to spend as a complete family. My father's youngest sister, Aunt Winnie, staying with friends at Loxwood, came over to join us before returning to her home in Sheffield. We all listened to King George the Sixth's broadcast, phrased in his slow intense voice, quoting the poem which has since become famous.

"And I said to the man who stood at the gate of the year,
'Give me a light that I may tread softly into the unknown.'
And he replied 'Go out into the darkness and put your
hand into the hand of God—
That shall be to you better than light.
And safer than a known way.'"

1940 dawned with military personnel increasing sharply. No bombs had been dropped but the R.A.F. were dropping leaflets over Germany. Officers were being billeted in local houses and the younger members of the local community were being pressed to organise dances, largely for Canadian officers, now in their hundreds, occupying the Canadian quarters in Bordon under their unusual geographical names, Quebec, South Louisburg, Martinique, Guadaloupe and St. Lucia. We formed a dance committee and many were the dances we were to attend during the next months, reminiscent of my "débutante" days in London now ten years in the past. Nearly all the Canadian officers were married men so it was less then wise to take much notice of their flattery or to take their amorous advances seriously.

In addition to lending their houses for dances and social gatherings, some patriotic householders had clubbed together to start a series of canteens for the troops now pouring into the Liphook, Headley and Grayshott area.

My father, constantly in London, often lunched at the Carlton Club, still in Pall Mall but later to be destroyed by Hitler's bombs, where he ran into old colleagues. We were interested in the scraps of information he brought home to Kirklands. Mr. Churchill, it seemed, restless against inaction, was said to be bombarding Mr. Chamberlain with imaginative plans for the pursuit of the war effort. The Prime Minister, a man of peace, appeared to be incapable of decisive action and muddled on. The French, it was being said, had little support from their countrymen and hoped to keep the war as far from French soil as possible.

Soviet Russia remained an enigma: the Nazi-Soviet pact remained firm. Very little news was being received from Soviet sources. As the weeks passed with so little happening, the British War Cabinet had started to become discredited with the public feeling disheartened. Mr. Churchill had sensed this mood.

Like many others, I, too, had begun to feel frustrated and bored. I wrote to an old friend, who, like me, was waiting to join the Services. "Go to the F.A.N.Y. headquarters," she wrote back, forwarding their address, "At the moment they have more volunteers than they need, but the situation may change." At the beginning of February it happened that "The Society of Women Writers and Journalists" of which my mother was president, was holding a lunch at the Forum Club in Halkin Street on the subject of "Women writers and the war". My mother was not well enough to travel but asked if I might attend the lunch as her representative which was kindly granted. Accordingly, I caught the train from Haslemere to Waterloo, petrol was far too precious to use for a journey of this sort, and enjoyed the lunch with many of my mother's old friends. I knew most of the members, having attended so many functions of this kind accompanying my mother in the pre-war years. It was a brief gathering, many members living outside London were more than anxious to get home before dark. This gave me ample time to find my way to the F.A.N.Y. headquarters and to put my name on their waiting list. The officer in charge stressed that it might be some months before they could make use of me but that she would keep my name and address before her. It was not encouraging, but at least I had made the first step. "You can always 'phone and we will let you know how things are moving," she told me.

I paid a brief visit to my own club, the Ladies' Carlton, opposite the Forum, and went to look at the swimming bath, now empty of water. It had been the scene of so much activity in the pre-war days when I had taken part in so many swimming galas. As chairman of the relevant committee it had also been my lot to tackle the organising, and hard work it was!

The light was now fading from the sky in this short February afternoon, and by the time I had walked through the parks and crossed Westminster Bridge it was quite dark. One could hear the cries of the newsvendors but one could not see them, causing a sensation of eeriness. On buying an evening paper it was necessary to crouch under a canopy shielding a hooded lantern to find the right coin. Traffic moved in a ghost-like way, their headlights thin points of light, queer phantoms, looming up and disappearing into the now almost solid darkness. The inside of Waterloo Station was so black it resembled a cave. My father and I had undertaken to meet and we managed to find each other on the right platform. Alighting at Haslemere, we drove home together in my car, smaller, easier to park, and with less petrol consumption than my father's larger Ford. Inside our blacked-out cottage, when we reached home, such a different home from 2 Cowley Street, but much appreciated, there was light, warmth, my mother's affectionate welcome, which never failed, and a cheerful exchange of family news.

March opened, bringing great discontent in France, M. Daladier's government had fallen, replaced by M. Reynaud, thought to be a more resolute man. British public opinion continued to show restlessness and frustration and there was contempt for Mr. Chamberlain's remark in Parliament, "Hitler has missed the bus".

CHAPTER TWO

Hitler, however, was right on target. On the night of the 8th April with breathless suddenness the German forces took over Denmark and proceeded to occupy every Norwegian port from Narvik to Oslo, moving ahead rapidly to surround the airfields. Wild confusion reigned, and in the British War Cabinet, it was afterwards admitted that the Admiralty and the War Office had been issuing contradictory orders. In their attempt to help the Norwegians the Allies failed disastrously. It was not surprising, therefore, that, in the opening days of May, the country's wrath turned against Mr. Chamberlain, still tainted by his reputation as an appeaser. Mr. Churchill, on the other hand, had stood alone for years calling out his solitary warnings.

There was uproar in Parliament, followed by much hesitancy and uncertainty behind the scenes. Lord Halifax had been suggested as Prime Minister to follow Mr. Chamberlain but he was not a young man and he adroitly extricated himself on the grounds that a Prime Minister could not be a peer. The veteran statesman Mr. Lloyd George together with many others, insisted, against some opposition, that Mr. Churchill alone, a great master of eloquence and experience, was the only possible leader who could command the country's support at such a time. Advised by a desperate Mr. Chamberlain, the King sent for Mr. Churchill. At the same moment the Germans invaded Holland and Belgium.

Mr. Churchill addressed the nation in the now famous and historical words, "I have nothing to offer but blood, toil, tears and sweat." A new spirit of optimism swept the land. It was to be a shimmering summer against the background of devastating news. In five days, with the Germans fiercely bombing Rotterdam, the Dutch capitulated. Queen Wilhelmina was forced to flee the country, first setting up a kind of Court in England, later taking her daughters to Canada. In return the R.A.F. bombed the Ruhr.

For a very short time, in Belgium, the allies held their own but when the Germans took Amiens and reached the sea the allied troops were cut off. With Belgium vanquished, Hitler turned his attention to the Maginot Line, supposedly impregnable. With German forces roaring into France, French morale collapsed. Goering now claimed that his Luftwaffe could destroy the British without effort and Mr. Churchill warned the nation to prepare for "hard and heavy tidings" while flying to France himself to persuade M. Reynaud to join in with the British, determined to fight on. Paris had now been reached and the veteran Marshal Pétain was talking of armistice.

Mussolini now chose this moment to throw in his lot with Hitler certain that German victory was assured. Mr. Churchill's resolute spirit reached new peaks and his inimitable speeches made the brilliant evacuation of Dunkirk, so well known in history, seem like a victory. But there were indeed "hard and heavy tidings". With the campaign of the "Low Countries" ended and Hitler in Paris, it became obvious that the invasion of Britain would begin. The "phoney war" was no more. German subjects in England were rapidly interned. Lest the enemy should arrive by parachute, road signs were removed and names of railway stations painted out; even booksellers were asked to destroy maps. Food rationing was tightened.

Soon a volunteer force to protect the public was being assembled first called "Local Defence Volunteers" but later changed to the much pleasanter name of "Home Guard". More than a million older men enrolled, all over the country, many of them veterans of the First World War. Their equipment was non-existent. And now Lord Beaverbrook, the new Minister of Munitions was calling for scrap metal. In every part of the land railings were being taken up and patriotic housewives were collecting their aluminium kitchen utensils and pots and pans. Mr. Churchill's constant message "Action *this* day" was beginning to stir even the most lethargic.

There was much talk of sending many children to America or to Canada and when Mr. Churchill went to give his report to the King in Buckingham Palace he was to find the King in the garden practising revolver shooting.

"Don't you think, Sir," he is reputed to have said, "That the two Princesses should be sent to a place of safety away from these

Islands?''

The answer came from the Queen.

''Mr. Prime Minister, the children can't go without me, I can't leave the King, and the King won't go.''

An officer called Charles de Gaulle had now arrived in London. He had taken on the title of ''Free French'' and many others were thought to be supporting him. We had lost France, but there were Poles, Norwegians, Dutch, Czechs, Belgians, and now French clamouring to join the common cause.

It was now clear that the whole British Expeditionary Force had been rescued from Dunkirk but with the loss of virtually all equipment.

Mr. Ernest Bevin, the Minister of Labour, a big man of great determination, had begun to inspire a new spirit in the factory workers. Guns, tanks, rifles, destroyers and aircraft all had to be replaced and with all possible speed.

Immense fortifications of jagged barbed-wire and other obstacles were being prepared all along the south and east coastline. Civil defence authorities had announced that church bells would be sounded to warn the population of airborne enemy troops.

The Prime Minister was now in private correspondence with President Roosevelt, a growing friendship of cardinal importance resulting in what was to become known as ''Lease-Lend''. The United States were painfully aware of Britain's peril, many indeed were beginning to express grave doubts as to the country's survival. The President desperately hoped to remain neutral as the U.S. was in no way equipped for war, but he was to arrange that certain arms designated as ''surplus'' could be transferred to the British as a gesture of admiration and sympathy. He was even to add a box or two of cigars!

A few rifles were beginning to find their way to the Home Guard, many of whom were now gathering to drill nightly, dressed in a whole variety of uniforms. Reports were circulating that much of the British Fleet had returned from the Mediterranean to home waters. The Germans had begun their bombing of convoy shipping.

We were soon to reach the decisive turning point of the war.

Meanwhile, my father and I redoubled our efforts in our vegetable garden and my mother continued with her indefatigable sewing. We worried a great deal about her health but we never mentioned it. I was still tied to my four-hour shifts in the ambulance telephone box and we had all passed our first aid and home nursing examinations which had been quite strict.

Goering had always exaggerated the strength of his Luftwaffe. On 13th August the Germans began their full attack on South-East England with fleets of bombers protected by fighters. The British had two great assets, in addition to the immense courage of their pilots, Air Marshal Dowding, and the instrument of radar. Hitler was certain that air attack would soon wear down British defences. A devastating attack was now to take place along the south coast with the Germans determined to destroy the fighter bases in Kent. They almost succeeded as British losses were appalling, but the German losses were greater. Hitler was now in a hurry, he needed to bring about a collapse of the British spirit before the advent of unfavourable autumn weather. He ordered Goering to turn the Luftwaffe aside and to bomb London. This bombing caused many civilian casualties and disrupted life but it saved the Kent airfields.

The country now believed that the crisis had come. "Instant readiness," we were told. The Home Guard had been informed that hundreds of barges had been accumulated along hostile coasts. The message "Cromwell" came out which meant "Invasion imminent" and in a few places the church bells sounded. We were all tense with nerves, but nothing happened.

The Luftwaffe now made another gigantic effort and on 15th September the brilliant pilots of the R.A.F. beat them back. They were shot down in high numbers overcome by gallantry and superiority. Fighter Command had triumphed. The whole nation felt swollen with pride. The Prime Minister expressed the country's gratitude. With his unique gift for words he expressed it simply, "Never in the field of human conflict was so much owed by so many to so few." The invasion had been repelled.

That winter of 1940-41 was to be a testing time. The enemy began to concentrate on night bombing. London came under severe attack but by November the bombers had turned their attention to industrial centres and ports.

I made a further visit to the F.A.N.Y. headquarters, determined to play a much more active part in the war effort.

"Many changes are taking place," I was told.

"We have now been taken over by the War Office and incorporated into the A.T.S."

"How much difference does that make?" I asked.

"Well it means that matters are out of our hands but we can still forward your name. Drivers are plentiful at the moment but we hear there is a shortage of clerical workers. Can you type and write shorthand?"

I had taught myself to type in a haphazard and not very efficient way before the war but I had never studied shorthand. Obviously this would need to be my next move. There were now many more ambulance drivers than the district required and I sought the Civil Defence authority to resign. Knowing that I now wished to join up the request was granted.

Searching through local advertisements I chanced upon the name of Mrs. L., who took a few pupils in shorthand and typewriting in a house in Farnham. I made contact immediately and became enrolled for her December class which was just commencing. I travelled to Farnham every day by 'bus and was soon engrossed. Mrs. L. seemed something of an amateur and lessons in typewriting were almost non-existent but as it was shorthand I had come to master I did not fuss.

We spent a very quiet Christmas, my mother overwhelmingly thankful, as indeed we all were, that my brother had got through the "Battle of Britain" and was now in the Air Ministry. His family had moved south to join him.

At the end of December an appalling incendiary raid had broken out over London. Hundreds of fires raged, water mains burst, and the sky, even as far away as Headley was flashing all round the horizon. We could see the sinister glow like a flaming sunset. The sirens in near-by areas appeared to be continuous . . . a new hazard, we were told, delayed action bombs. In the lurid light it looked as if half London must be derelict and burning.

My father, on his return from London, described the tragic scenes, soon to become familiar in many centres, charred and burning buildings, acres of twisted girders, streets ankle-deep in rubble, water streaming along unchecked, shattered brickwork and splintered glass. Despite this misery, the country's morale remained high. Life went on even if some of the boarded up offices and shops appeared to be tenanted by ghosts.

Shaking the rubble out of their bomb-damaged clothes, brave citizens all over the country carried on their lives with infinite resource and fortitude. It was even rumoured that the "ladies of the night" unable to seek out customers in the black-out had taken to shining torches on to their own faces, to the utter horror of the Air Raid Wardens.

A few courageous bomb stories were being circulated. They ran as follows:

An elderly lady asked by a country friend how she could endure remaining in London under heavy bombardment gave this reply, "I wait until darkness, then I make my cup of Horlicks, not rationed yet, climb into bed, read my bible for an hour, pull the covers over my head and declare 'To hell with the swine!'"

The second related to a cockney Londoner caught in an air raid centre, a deep shelter close to the River Thames. There had been a particularly savage raid causing part of the river wall to be breached and the water was rising. A shrill voice announced, "Well, I brought me gas mask. I brought me ration book, I brought me identity card, I brought me purse, but I'm . . . if I brought me water wings!"

There was not much to laugh at through that bitter winter but it was reported that the King delighted in being addressed by Mr. Ernest Bevin, the Minister of Labour, as "me lad" and that Queen Mary had laughed gaily on being told of Mr. Bevin's remark on sampling his first helping of caviar, "This jam tastes fishy."

The factory workers, despite the interruption of air raids and inspired by Mr. Bevin were rapidly replacing the heavy loss of weapons left behind at Dunkirk.

CHAPTER THREE

In May 1941 the crackle of incendiaries and thunderous roar of guns and high explosives reached a new climax. News was released that the Debating Chamber of the House of Commons had been demolished. I went again to London to have another talk with the officer at the F.A.N.Y. headquarters who informed me that my name had gone through to the War Office.

The Ladies' Carlton was still intact although a bomb had destroyed the swimming bath. In Cowley Street bomb blast had badly damaged one part of our former home while the house opposite had received a direct hit and was in ruins. London was a tragic sight, as also were Coventry, Plymouth, Southampton, Sheffield, Hull and many more. It was no longer one-way traffic however, the British were making retaliatory raids over Germany. So far these appalling raids with their rising casualties had not dented the indomitable British spirit.

Quite suddenly, at the end of May, I received instructions from the War Office to report for a medical examination at an Army Hospital in Salisbury. At last I was on my way. In an outer office of this enormous building I was duly asked to sign my name at the foot of many documents, later taking my place in a queue of many other women awaiting the medical exam. In due course a certificate was filled in and stamped A.W.I. The "W" I was later to discover stood for "Woman" and cropped up with one's army number and many other details, all through one's A.T.S. career.

A week later another letter reached me with instructions to report to a former girls' school called Beaufront, now No. 1 M.T.T.C. Camberley. I was given the date, 10th June, 1941.

M.T.T.C. translated as Motor Transport Training Centre, and I had been requested to report as a "clerk" to the Administrative Headquarters. Now that the date was actually in front, I felt very nervous. My shorthand, although I had worked hard, was barely up to standard after only five months, and my typing, although accurate, remained self-taught. Mrs. L's tuition had been of very little value from the typing angle. I was now committed, however, and could not back down.

My dear mother embroidered my dressing-gown with sprigs of white heather for good luck. I had been informed that "Other Ranks", as I was now to be called, might retain that one garment, although all other clothing was obligatory in "Army Issue". One great blessing was the permission to retain the use of my car, provided that I had the petrol coupons. This boon was reported to me by the F.A.N.Y. officer in Aldershot who had interviewed me a day or two previously. She also told me that I would be permitted to wear the F.A.N.Y. shoulder "flashes", which, as she explained, "will not be a great deal of use to you now that we are all under the A.T.S. and run by the War Office, but they may lead to a certain 'camaraderie' among your fellows."

The family gave me a wonderful send-off party with my R.A.F. brother joining us for one night, and our treasured cook surpassing herself with our garden vegetables and dried eggs. I felt torn with conflicting emotions, deeply worried about my mother's ill-health,

Plate 2

Hitler and Goering inspecting the Richthofen Squadron.

which she hid so bravely, and my determination to play a bigger part in the war.

I waved goodbye, looking back to the rose-pink ramblers, blue lavender and orange marigolds against their background of honeysuckle and tall feathery grasses, with a feeling of deep apprehension and uncertainty.

There were no signposts and I did not know the Camberley area, but the kindly officer at Aldershot had described the position of "Beaufront" the former girls' school. I found a pleasant drive of sycamores, chestnuts and ash and drove in to find myself confronting a red-brick, rather Victorian-looking building. Parking my car under some trees, I left my suitcase and timidly pushed open a front door which appeared to be ajar.

There was not a soul to be seen. Much surprised, I walked round—no one. There was, however, considerable feminine chatter emanating from a room marked "Permanent Staff". Very nervously I peeped in. The room was filled with young women in khaki uniforms. They eyed me in silence. Had I done something terrible, I wondered. Suddenly, a round-faced corporal wearing a hat, with a red scarf around her shoulder, came forward to meet me.

"Are you a new student?" she asked. "The intake isn't due until tomorrow, you've come a day early." I explained that I had been posted as a "clerk" showing her my War Office letter.

"Oh! I see," she replied. "Well, I'm afraid you'll have to wait for some time, there's a great flap on, a W.O. Inspection, red braid and all that. The brass hats are all together at the moment inspecting Crawley Rise." Crawley Rise might have been in China for all the sense it conveyed, but I was soon to learn that it was, in fact, a commandeered private house serving as the Training Centre's Administrative Headquarters. Thanking the corporal, I withdrew feeling very embarrassed. But what to do next? A clock chimed three. I sat down on a bench in the school hall.

The friendly corporal reappeared carrying an immense mug of tea and a huge sticky bun.

"I expect you'd like some tea," she said. Thanking her warmly I plucked up courage to ask "You mentioned 'students', what does that actually mean?"

"Well, all the trainee-drivers are called students for want of a better name. As you know this is a Motor Transport Training Centre. They come in for a month and then those who pass are sent on to companies, the failures have to change category and become either orderlies or cooks.''

"Do many fail?" I queried.

"It varies tremendously, but of course this Training Centre has only been in existence for less than a year.''

I was grateful for her kindness and on handing her back the mug agreed with her advice. "It may be hours before the inspection ends, why don't you go out and look around a bit?''

From an old map in my car I found my way into the town centre of Camberley about two miles from the school. On that long-ago June afternoon, forty years ago, it was very quiet. There were a few women shoppers and one or two girls pushing babies in prams. The High Street was almost deserted. I found the Post Office, went in and took a telegraph form. My parents were eager for news so I filled in the one word "Vix". This was a family code meaning "Thumbs up—I'm all right", which members of my family often communicated with each other in times of stress, or if separated by long distances. My father had used it frequently from 1915-1917 when he had been engaged in secret service work in the U.S.A.

The code had been evolved by my mother's father, Sir Robert Harvey, our beloved grandfather, and the family had carried it on. The girl behind the wire grill took the form with the query, "Is that all?''

"Yes," I replied, "It's a code.'' My stock seemed to rise.

"I'll get it off at once," she added.

I walked round the town, so much smaller in those days, and found the railway station. Posters abounded "Careless talk costs lives" and "Be like Dad, keep Mum''. In due course I felt it might be wise to return to Beaufront. On this second occasion, I parked my car for the night and pulled out my suitcase. Now it was a changed scene, young women in khaki were everywhere and there was a good deal of noise. The round-faced corporal, still wearing the red sash, came towards me.

"Sergeant B. is looking for you," she told me. At the same moment a brisk rather masculine woman with three stripes on her sleeve bore down upon me.

"Are you Brittain?" she questioned. I replied that I was.

"You should not have gone out again once you had reported," she admonished. I made no comment. "Well, take your case and I'll show you where you're sleeping. It's Room 4. What made you choose the wrong day?" Once again I pulled out my letter of instructions from the War Office. Handing it back she commented, "Oh! I see, you've been *posted* here, you are not a student. I thought it odd that you should have come by car. Well, in any case, you will have to go through the month's course with the students whose intake starts tomorrow." I followed her up a wide staircase and into an obvious girls' school dormitory where there were five beds.

After taking down my particulars: christian names, age, home address, religion and names of next-of-kin, she gave me instructions. "You'll be in A Squad and I'm your sergeant. My name's B. You'll be alone tonight but tomorrow four students will join you. Choose any bed you like. The biscuits and pillows are stacked, also blankets. Sheets will not be issued until tomorrow. Your army issue clothing will be given to you as soon as the other students arrive. Carry your civilian gas mask for the moment. The baths and chloras are at the end of the corridor. Supper is at 19.30 and you'll hear a bell." As briskly as she had appeared, the sergeant vanished.

Biscuits? Chloras? I mused. What astonishing names! A bell clanged harshly. That was obviously supper. Following a number of khaki-clad girls down a long passage I entered an oblong school dining-room filled with scrubbed wooden tables and wooden benches. At the far end stood girls in white overalls, together with an officer wearing a red sash, presiding over enormous kitchen dishes. The A.T.S. girls wore army respirators slung over their shoulders from which they were producing cutlery. This, I was to learn later, was disallowed, but the officers usually turned a blind eye. Where else could one carry one's personal cutlery? Naturally I had no cutlery and wondered how I was going to manage. Suddenly I recognised one of the girls who had been on the Headley Dance Committee. She had arrived at Beaufront a month ahead of me. With great kindness she came to my aid. "Have my spoon," she urged, "I can manage with a fork. You'll get your issue tomorrow. It's cottage pie and jam tart." I was more than grateful. "Tell me the Headley news," she pressed.

CHAPTER FOUR

The morning sunshine danced into my lone school dormitory the following morning as I rose from my uncomfortable bed. I looked out at the chequered woodlands around the school building, emerald, olive and jade, so fresh in the early light, now a completely built up area. Soon a bell clanged noisily and I took my place in the breakfast queue, standing out like the proverbial "sore thumb" the only individual in a cotton dress amidst all the uniforms. As I passed the orderly officer she handed me a knife and fork with the command, "Wash them and take them back to the pantry, get someone to show you where it is." I felt very relieved, not knowing how I was going to tackle my sausages and tomatoes, and a giant doorstep of bread decorated with a dollop of marmalade, without my own cutlery. The gigantic mug of tea appeared again, looking to my unaccustomed eyes the size of a flower-pot. My Headley friend was late so I did not see her.

Suddenly Sergeant B. appeared behind me. "Be in the main hall at 8.30 sharp," she ordered, "And Corporal P. will take you over to Crawley Rise." She vanished again. She must have "Cheshire Cat" qualities I thought.

A little later the said Corporal P., a pleasant, tall girl in her early twenties, led me across the broad span of grass which must have served as the girls' school playground, into a large house on the opposite side of the main road. On the way she gave me useful details of the whole Training Centre. "Beaufront is only one of three," she explained, "The other two are called Cordwalles and Mulroy, all within half a mile radius from Crawley Rise."

They are known as 1, 2 and 3 Companies. Beaufront is 1. Cordwalles was a boys' prep. school, Mulroy was another girls' school. On reaching Crawley Rise, we climbed some back stairs until we arrived at a landing faced by three doors marked C.O., Adjutant and Q.M. Being totally ignorant of all army jargon and initials, C.O. seemed to suggest Conscientious Objector.

Knocking on the adjutant's door, Corporal P. pushed me into the room with the announcement, "Private Brittain, Ma'am,

Plate 3

My two-year-old niece, Alida, at the time of Mr. Chamberlain's fateful broadcast.

Plate 4

Aunt Winnie, Mrs. F. W. Ellwood, in the doorway of her hospitable Sheffield home.

Clerk." The adjutant continued writing for a moment. Then looking up, she gave me a most welcoming smile, rose from her chair, and approached me with outstretched hand. To my surprise she exclaimed, "You're Lady Brittain's daughter! I would have known you anywhere. I worked for years in Palace Chambers, Bridge Street, next door to your mother's office, the National Conservative Musical Union. How lovely to have you with us. I believe you're a speaker, aren't you? Weren't you a Primrose League Gold Medallist?" I replied that I was, in fact, a fairly experienced speaker, but added that I feared I was an extremely inexperienced "clerk". "Well, never mind," she continued.

"We'll use you in Records to begin with and then see how it goes. Tell me, how is your dear mother and how is Sir Harry?"

The interview was interrupted by her telephone. I felt immensely encouraged to feel that at least one officer knew me and withdrew to the landing. A very severe looking young woman passed me. "That's the R.S.M.," said Corporal P., reappearing. "What does that mean?" I queried. "Regimental Sergeant Major. Are you to go to Records? I'll take you." In a top floor room, another friendly corporal greeted me. This room seemed to be a hive of activity and the sound of clattering typewriters nearly deafening.

The records office was utterly bewildering and by the end of the day I felt worn out and apologised to Corporal H. for all the work I was giving her. "Don't worry," she answered. "I was just as green and much slower, you grasp things quickly." Walking back to the main school building I felt that the adjutant's connection with my mother had been an unforeseen piece of good fortune. At least, now, I was on the bottom rung.

That night there were five of us in Room No. 4, and, much to my relief, sheets had been issued. We eyed one other with some interest. We were an odd assortment, one girl of nineteen was from the "horsey" background of Warwickshire, crazy about horses; a second was a sensible mid-twenties secretary to a London firm of solicitors; a third a cockney hairdresser, and the fourth a young waitress from Glasgow who was very difficult to understand. Strangely enough, we all got along splendidly. The secretary became one of my best friends and we kept in touch for many years.

In modern jargon the next days were "All go". We were hurtled around in army trucks for every kind of inspection, heart, lungs, blood-pressure, teeth, feet, even hair. "You are in the top category, A.W.1.," the medical officer told me, "But you will need to be careful about catching cold, you might easily get bronchial." This had been a weakness since my childhood tonsils operation when I had suffered from anaesthetic inhalation, as it was called, and I gave the medical officer high marks for noticing it. For some reason there was no eyesight or hearing test which one would have regarded as important for potential drivers. Our little "horsey" companion expressed relief. "I can't see a foot!" she declared. It was not for us to give her away.

After the tough medical inspection we were lined up in the quartermaster's stores to be issued with army uniforms and all other clothing, together with camouflaged steel helmets, army respirators and haversacks. It was now forbidden to use the civilian terms "tin hats" and "gas masks". Then Sergeant B. shepherded us back to Room 4 with instructions that all buttons, buckles and shoes were to be polished to shine like glass.

Soon we were mustered together for instruction in army etiquette. Hats had to be withdrawn immediately on entering a building but were obligatory at all other times. Saluting of all officers was compulsory but could not be carried out without wearing a hat. All personal possessions had to be carried in the pockets of our khaki jackets and we were strongly advised to sew additional pockets on the inside of our skirts. Slacks would not be issued except for drivers and could not be worn off duty. Every garment had to be marked with the owner's name. It all seemed reminiscent of one's schooldays.

On our second morning we were given typhoid and tetanus injections which had a devastating effect. In addition to extremely sore arms many of us felt really ill. Happily, the ghastly sensation wore off in twenty-four hours.

No sooner had we recovered from this horrible experience than we were given an "I.Q." test. This involved answering a host of puzzles, filling in missing words, giving the answers to general knowledge questions, adding and subtracting figures, drawing curious diagrams and other oddities, all at top speed. I felt extraordinarily pleased when Sergeant B. informed me, "You've done very well, best squad result I've had so far."

CHAPTER FIVE

The days ran on. In mid-June the whole of the south of England became caught up in a sweltering heatwave. We were allowed to go into "shirt sleeve order" as it was called, provided our sleeves were not rolled any higher than the elbows. This new order had its hazards. Jackets had to be left hanging on chairs and this meant easy access to the contents of pockets for those with pilfering in mind. Alas, there were many light-fingered recruits even in the days of volunteers. The compulsory call-up of women was some months away at that time. To overcome this, several of us bought little bags from Woolworths which we tied around our waists under our skirt bands. These were apt to make an ugly bulge, but understanding A.T.S. officers tended not to have seen it.

At the end of our first fortnight a new hazard emerged. The compulsion of attendance at N.A.A.F.I. dances. There were innumerable army units, many rescued from Dunkirk, stationed in the Aldershot, Farnborough, Frimley, Pirbright and Camberley area who appeared to be in need of feminine company at their Saturday evening N.A.A.F.I. dances. We were not invited, we were "detailed" to attend these functions, rounded up rather like cattle and herded into army lorries transported hither and thither in the Hampshire and Surrey countryside. The dances were not popular, becoming rugged, very hot and rather rowdy but we tolerated them as being all part of our war effort. Our weekly pay of 11/6d. a week, about 57p, did not run to heavy drinking, even in those days. Luckily our return, like Cinderella, took place at midnight, so we were spared any excessive high spirits said to have taken place by some of the troops after our departure.

I was working in the records office during the mornings, typing out immense documents which were known as "bird-cages", but in the afternoons I joined my "student" colleagues for the interminable lectures on anti-gas precautions, first aid, map reading, convoy driving, and general car maintenance.

A sergeant from Sandhurst had come over to give us gas drill. Our normal drill took place early, grass-bashing as it was called. When we had reached a good enough standard we were allowed to drill at Sandhurst with an army band which we all found quite exhilarating. But much less pleasant was the sampling of gas chambers when we had to stand unprotected for two minutes with choking lungs.

On 21st June I was given my first 48 hours leave pass which I welcomed joyfully. It was, in fact, my birthday weekend. Kirklands had never seemed lovelier. We sat under the copper beech admiring my father's superb herbaceous border of phlox, antirrhinums, campanula, and larkspur. My mother, ever sewing, but always for others, was eager to learn of my experiences.

But the war was not far away. We could still hear the wailing sirens and the sound of gunfire.

On the morning of 22nd June, listening to the news on our cottage wireless, as it was still called, we received the startling information that the Germans had invaded Soviet Russia. The Prime Minister broadcast that evening, "The Russian danger is now our danger, and the danger of the United States." The great fear of communism, acute for many years, would now have to be put aside with Russia as our ally. The war was to bring some strange "bedfellows".

By this time, June 1941, many Londoners had set up their abode nightly in the Underground Stations. The Ministry of Health were sending inspectors, and Lord Woolton, the Minister of Food, was endeavouring to maintain the highest standard possible for the nation's food supply. Even so, civilian rations were extremely meagre and I was more than grateful to be allowed to collect army rations to take to my family when I was granted leave.

A Consumer Needs Department had now been established to discover the most urgent shortages. A new "Utility" label had been devised for clothes, blankets, certain materials and furniture. Rationing had now been turned into a system of "points" allowing individuals a certain amount of choice.

The bombing of London and many other cities continued. After severe raids, the indomitable King and Queen visited the worst areas. After Buckingham Palace had been hit by a bomb the Queen made her now well-known statement, "I'm glad we've been bombed, I feel I can look the East End in the face."

The Prime Minister, too, found time to visit the bombed areas, often deeply moved by the people's bravery. Morale remained high. The British still regarded themselves as a Great Power. In their minds, the possibility of defeat was quite unthinkable. The common danger had cemented national unity.

We were now approaching the time which was to become known as "The Battle of the Atlantic" when countless thousands of tons of shipping were to be tragically sunk by German U-boats.

July remained swelteringly hot and my poor fellow "students" were all in a state of anxiety about passing their respective driving tests. I had also been called upon to take a most exacting clerk's exam requiring immense concentration. But, notwithstanding our worries, we felt glad to be in uniform. It made us feel much more involved in the war effort. Life at Camberley was wonderfully free, after working hours. We were permitted to go anywhere we chose and many of us enjoyed sampling the numerous attractive cafés and restaurants which were dotted around the area in those days. There were also four cinemas to choose from, all with good programmes. The best seats cost no more than 1/6d. now 7½p. Certainly it was not "La vie en rose" but, looking back, it was a very worthwhile experience.

On the last day of the course, the adjutant sent for me. "You are getting the hang of things splendidly," she told me. "So far, you are our best I.Q. candidate, but I want to put you on the telephone switchboard for a fortnight or so to give you more experience." I replied that I had never before worked a telephone switchboard but would certainly do my best to master it.

The switchboard, pushed away in a tiny little box of a room was absolute bedlam. Innumerable calls came in simultaneously and had to be held back, and as most of the callers spoke only in army jargon, or army initials I was frequently quite unable to understand them. It felt like grappling with a foreign language! But, in time, I began to get on top of it.

My fellow "students" all passed the driving test and were posted to different companies. I was sent into Red Lodge, at the foot of Beaufront drive, to share a bedroom with M., a fellow clerk from the records office. We were to have some happy times for a few months.

CHAPTER SIX

The great harvest moon was now hanging low over the elm trees, and in the soft light of late August, my brother and I drove through a few ribbons of mist. He was returning me to Red Lodge after we had had a meal together to celebrate his promotion to Wing Commander. He had been in Farnborough carrying out some R.A.F. duties. I had admired the charming photographs of the two children, now aged four and two. The family were shortly to take up residence in Rickmansworth as my brother was to return again to the Air Ministry. Like me, he had visited our former London home, 2 Cowley Street, and had been shocked by the damage. "What a lucky thing you pressed us all to find Kirklands," I told him.

The country's need for American help had now become urgent and the news had been released that the Prime Minister had carried out the first of his many meetings at sea with President Roosevelt. Together they had drawn up the Atlantic Charter. There had been huge defeats and catastrophic losses on the Russian front but the Russians were holding firm. The U.S.A. were determined to remain neutral.

In No. 1 M.T.T.C. at Camberley, September was to be a month of unceasing exertion. It was a time of War Office inspections, constant respirator drill in marching order, fire drill, first aid exercises, additional injections for typhoid and vaccination for smallpox, enormous extra work in the records office and repeated night duty. We certainly earned our few hours off at the week-ends, and some of us managed to hitch a lift to London to see a matinée. The theatres were flourishing.

I was lucky enough to spend many Sundays at Kirklands where my hospitable parents encouraged me to bring friends. I could never have considered these visits without army rations.

In October my life was to take a new turn. I was on late clerk's duty and had gone in to the adjutant to get her to sign a final batch of letters, when she asked me to sit down.

"I want to put a proposal to you," she said. "I know you are an experienced speaker so I have been wondering if you would consider helping us out here with some of the lecturing?" Taken completely by surprise I answered truthfully, "I would like to try very much." She then continued, "I have seen the exam results you took as a student, you did remarkably well. It would be an immense help to have another 'ready made' lecturer." "When should I begin?" I queried.

"Well, straight away, if you will. Of course you will have to start as a private but we plan to make you a corporal as soon as there is a squad vacancy. This will probably be in about a fortnight when Sergeant W. leaves to go for her commission. That will allow Corporal T. to be promoted and we can fit you in there." With a warm smile she continued, "You will need to carry on as a clerk as long as you remain a private so it will be extremely hard work, but I am sure you are equal to it." I remarked that I greatly appreciated being singled out and would certainly do the best I could. "I knew we could rely on you. And do tell me, how is your dear mother? You must remember me to her next time you go home."

Pushing the newly signed letters into their respective envelopes I certainly felt very elated, a corporal's pay was quite good! One had to bear in mind the standard of the time.

Plate 5

Fishing on Lake Tarawera, Uncle Bob, Colonel W. B. Brittain, whose abundant food parcels from New Zealand were so warmly appreciated.

CHAPTER SEVEN

My first full week's leave was due. I spent a night or two at my club in London before joining my parents. The terrible debris and trail of desolation now lay right across London and I was appalled to see the damage to old Westminster Hall and to our familiar church, St. John's, Smith Square, now lying in a heap of ruins. Even poor old Big Ben had not escaped, there was an ugly gash right across the stonework framing the blackened face. Unlike the First World War, when the clock had been silenced, the bells still struck the hour and chimed. The sound was reassuring.

After a day at Kirklands my father asked me if my mother and I would like to accompany him to a lunch at the Savoy given by a leading American broadcaster who was an old friend. He had saved enough petrol coupons to enable us to travel by car, and my mother, although frail, agreed that she would love to accompany us. Since the invasion of Russia the bombing had ceased. It was a great day.

Overlooking the silver scythe of the Thames our host proclaimed, "Well, this is Europe's 'night' but, believe me, you folk are far happier in this war-torn country than we are in the States, we feel shamed."

It was now clear that, despite great defeats and terrible losses the Germans had failed in their bid to overcome Russia and to reach the Caucasus. The British, however, were more cheerful, thanks to the Prime Minister's brave decision to send reinforcements round the Cape of Good Hope. The army were now in possession of an extensive area of Italian North Africa. Unfortunately, they were to lose this before the whole situation in North Africa was to become drastically altered. The enemy were being reinforced by the famous German tank commander General Rommel.

There was now a very sinister shadow in the Far East. In September 1940 Japan had joined the Rome-Berlin Axis and, with the consent of Vichy France, had moved troops into Indo-China. In April 1941 a pact of neutrality had been signed between Japan and Russia. The militant Japanese had seen the chance of acquiring a vast empire over China and the South-East, some believing it to be their destiny to lead the Asian people away from the power of the European West, Britain, Holland and France. In the view of the Japanese, the West had no right to the people of Asia or to their land.

To achieve their aim, however, the Japanese needed to destroy the American Fleet. The Japanese-manned aircraft had reached a remarkable degree of efficiency, and, on 7th December, 1941 they struck at Pearl Harbour dropping some thousands of tons of explosives sinking eight American battleships and many smaller vessels with the loss of more than two thousand casualties. This brutal assault awoke "The great sleeping giant" as America had been called, bringing the outraged U.S.A. into the war. In addition to declaring war against Japan, President Roosevelt declared war against Germany.

The great journalist Mr. J. L. Garvin wrote, "This is the world's fight for all time" and the Prime Minister proclaimed the famous phrase, "In the east the sun climbs slow, how slowly, but westward, look, the land is bright!"

The Japanese had struck great blows against the British in the Far East and now Singapore had fallen, and the battleship *Prince of Wales* and the battlecruiser *Repulse* had been lost. But the hard-pressed British were no longer fighting alone.

CHAPTER EIGHT

On my return from leave, my lecturing on the three subjects of gas, first aid and map reading started in earnest. As I was still a clerk in the records office the additional work was considerable and it was also something of an embarrassment to be in a position of authority while still a private.

After a month, however, my Beaufront company commander sent for me. "Your lectures are 'star quality'," she told me, very flatteringly, "And we are now promoting you to corporal. You will join your fellow corporals in Room 6 at No. 2 Company, Cordwalles, and you will be squad corporal in 'F' Squad. Congratulations." I was sorry to leave Red Lodge where my little friend M., a remarkably efficient typist, also in records, had been such an agreeable companion. In fact, matrimony was to claim her before the end of the war. She was the fastest typist I had ever met and superbly efficient, but after her marriage I lost touch.

Clearing my desk at last on my way to Cordwalles, I received a message from the adjutant.

"Well done, I knew you could do it. You're really raising sparks. I'm so glad we tapped this talent, we might have wasted you. Best of luck for the future." I expressed my thanks very gratefully. Had any other officer been adjutant at Crawley Rise in that autumn of 1941 I might have remained a very indifferent clerk throughout the war. And I doubt if my typing would have improved much—or my indifferent shorthand!

My new colleagues at Cordwalles greeted me with much kindness and the work of squad corporal proved to me infinitely more rewarding. Having found my feet, I was able to experiment quite boldly with some new lecturing approaches.

The heatwave summer and mild autumn were beginning to give way to a bitter winter with the early frosted trees resembling Christmas cards. On Christmas Eve I was allowed an afternoon off and drove over to Kirklands to take my family Christmas presents and to wish my father many happy returns for his 68th birthday. I had not been granted Christmas Day leave, but happily my brother was bringing his family to spend the few days holiday with our parents, which was to bring my mother great happiness. She doted on her two lovely grandchildren. My corporal stripes had brought them much pleasure.

Driving back into the little garage near Crawley Rise which some of us were now permitted to use, I became aware of a strong smell of burning. It was then that I noticed terrific flames shuddering and jumping above the Beaufront trees. The thick smoke was quite choking as I ran into the grounds now horror struck to see the entire building absolutely engulfed in flames. The whole lawn had become little more than a dumping ground with army and personal property, including the adjutant's poor terrified canary, stretching right across the width of the grass. In the background the N.C.O.s were feverishly moving the valuable cars, lorries and trucks from what was known as "the bays" well away from the danger of fire. Exhausted officers and A.T.S. from all three companies were struggling desperately to get Beaufront equipment cleared.

Joining the chain immediately, every hand counted, I helped to pass the furniture, kitchen utensils, bedding, linen, blankets, crockery and a host of other items to be stacked in the Nissen huts under the trees which were then in the process of being erected to augment future "intakes" of driver trainees.

The fire brigade were playing water all round the building but the roof had now caved in, slates were rocketing everywhere and the windows were cracking and splintering with a noise like fireworks. We had to keep diving away from blazing bits of roof which dropped near us, and water was now gushing along the paths in raging streams. To add to our difficulties a fierce wind had sprung up hurling blazing sparks into the sky. This was a fresh hazard as Beaufront was surrounded by trees.

At long last, with the whole building burnt out and only the walls left standing, the commandant insisted on a roll-call. No one was missing, even Satan, the Beaufront cat, was present, furious at the disturbance and even more put out at having to bed down with Figaro, our Red Lodge cat, as the two were known to be incompatible.

It then became necessary to make up an immense number of extra beds in Cordwalles and Mulroy and we all worked late into the night. We shared out as much as we could of our army clothing with those who had lost their possessions, and the gallant sergeant cooks managed to put on some kind of a meal. Finally, beds having been found for the displaced staff and students from Beaufront, the exhausted commandant with other officers looked in from room to room with the well worn words, "Happy Christmas, everyone." A burst of applause followed with the loud refrain "For they are jolly good fellows". Now it was Christmas morning and we all gathered in our night attire singing Christmas carols. "Bed," interrupted the hoarse company sergeant major, "Get to bed everybody, church parade at 9.30."

The first threads of daylight were already yellow in the eastern sky and the birds were stirring.

On Boxing Day the officers produced a magnificent performance of "Alice in Wonderland" greatly appreciated by the immensely enthusiastic audience. Our Christmas fare could not have been outclassed, and the sugar had been saved for months for the gigantic iced cake which we all shared. Satan and Figaro had been treated to a little taste of turkey!

A hard working E.N.S.A. company also paid us a visit and we all enjoyed a memorable version of Ivor Novello's *Fresh Fields*. Snow was now falling and it had begun to feel extremely cold. War news was scarce but we listened to the Prime Minister's broadcast, "We have done well, but we must do better." Many of us sat up to greet the New Year of 1942 and I was able to telephone my parents who expressed their great regret about the Beaufront fire. They had so much enjoyed the family Christmas with the grandchildren.

In mid-January a great surprise was in store. My "F" squad sergeant was suddenly called to attend an officer cadet training unit with a view to a commission. Then the company commander sent for me.

"I know this is a meteoric rise," she told me, "But we are promoting you to sergeant and you will take over 'F' Squad. Your lecturing is admirable and you have introduced a fresh breeze, in fact the students from your classes are reaching a higher standard in their exam results." I was extremely surprised but very pleased and thanked her warmly.

On collecting another lot of "stripes" from the quartermaster sergeant she exclaimed, "That's the quickest promotion I have known, you must be 'top of the league'."

By late January winter had really gripped the whole land. Icicles hung from the trees like glittering chandeliers and the whole countryside was hidden under a white blanket of snow. The driver trainees and their instructors were immobilised. There was a limit to the amount of time they could spend polishing their vehicles and sweeping snow. Then I had an idea.

How would they like a few talks, I wondered, on the enduring roots of our national life, the trials and tribulations of our forefathers, earlier years of endurance when scores of previous generations had been caught up in war? I put the suggestion to the company commander and she replied with enormous enthusiasm, "Why, how brilliant, do you think you can carry it out?"

I scraped my memory for the long-ago history lessons of my schooldays, working out a series: The Roman Occupation, the Danes and King Alfred, the Norman Invasion, Henry the Fifth and the Wars of the Roses, the Civil War, and if there was still time, Blenheim and Waterloo. Starting with my own squad I found others joined in, and before the snow melted, the onetime little boys' gymnasium at Cordwalles was crowded to the walls. In order to get the students to participate I suggested that we should have historical charades in the afternoons, an idea rapturously received. By the end of February a thaw set in and driving restarted: the students expressed disappointment!

My leave was due again and I spent a few days at Kirklands very much worried over my mother's breathlessness. The doctor told me that her heart was the chief cause. "She is warm and well looked after," he said, "And she would be horrified if you were to give up your A.T.S. career to come home now." But I felt deeply depressed on my return to Camberley.

Pearl Harbour had changed the course of the war. Britain and the United States had drawn closer together with the U.S. President and the Prime Minister declaring that they would wage war together in partnership, neither side making a separate peace or armistice with the enemy. The term Combined Chiefs of Staff had been born to become the pivot of this new united campaign. The balance of advantage had now tipped slightly in Britain's favour.

Hitler's troops were struggling desperately against Russia in a country solidly frozen by one of the cruellest winters of the century.

Many changes were now to take place on the home front. Full conscription for women had been introduced from eighteen to forty, rationing of food was to become tighter, soap needed to be most carefully conserved, bath water was to be restricted to no more than five inches in a bath, and restaurant meals were to be obliged to limit their charges to 5 shillings, 25p. The precious petrol

Plate 6

In Kirklands vegetable garden, my father making a start at "digging for victory".

coupons were also to be reduced, and coal was to be used very sparingly.

I was now sharing a small room with a fellow sergeant, over the cookhouse, which gave us welcome warmth. Our meals were of a very high standard and the pleasant camaraderie of the sergeants' mess, to say nothing of the prodigious status which three stripes provided, would have made my life very agreeable but for my increasing concern about my mother's ill health. My father's presence at Kirklands, however, was a great relief, and he had just published a book called *Pilgrim Partners* which was to lead to some worthwhile war work at a later date, and to Anglo-American broadcasting in which he excelled.

Something remarkably new was now to enter our A.T.S. lives. It was called A.B.C.A., Army Bureau of Current Affairs. We were to receive weekly pamphlets in the hope that the officers or senior N.C.O.s would organise discussions with the other ranks, gathering together for a half-hour exchange of views. The success or otherwise of these sessions depended entirely on those in charge and while some persuasive officers could pull out views from even the most reluctant, others failed abysmally. War news was difficult to follow, there was no television, transistor radios had not yet been invented, and there was a shortage of newspapers.

In London, lunch-time concerts were being organised in the National Gallery. For the time being, there was a brief rest from bombing, but Bomber Command had been gaining strength and was now bringing about some enormously dramatic raids on targets in Germany.

Very soon a board of senior A.T.S. officers arrived in Camberley from the War Office. All N.C.O.s were sent to be interviewed with the object of being selected for commissions. The new conscription of women had produced a great demand for potential officers.

"Would you be willing?" I was asked.

"Certainly," I replied, realising that our pleasant life in the Motor Transport Training Centre could not last indefinitely. "You will have the summer to make up your mind, but we think you will be urgently needed by the early autumn."

Winter was giving way to spring and we were beginning to work out convoy driving, very difficult with a total lack of signposts. The trainee drivers showed great enthusiasm.

CHAPTER NINE

One gusty March morning the company commander sent for me again. "There is to be a course on gas at Winterbourne Gunner, near Salisbury," she told me. "We hear it is very tough but we have to send a sergeant. Would you feel like tackling it? It is a fortnight's course but there is a carrot of a fortnight's leave to follow." Knowing that I had no choice, I naturally consented.

The journey to Winterbourne Gunner was difficult involving a number of train changes, but I arrived at length on a pouring wet evening and was met by an army truck at Salisbury. In due course other candidates joined me. We were driven, cold and dripping, into an army camp establishment in what appeared to be a complete wilderness. An A.T.S. officer met us. "Get off your wet things," she commanded, "And then go straight to supper in the sergeant's mess. Walk on the duck boards and follow the sign." We did as we were told. Later a sergeant led us to a series of Nissen huts where we were to sleep.

Then followed the most strenuous fortnight of all my A.T.S. experience. Every day we rose at 6.00 a.m., attending a non-stop stream of lectures, interrupted by parades dressed in army respirators and gas capes, forced to breathe what was then known as D.M. gas, afterwards running, utterly exhausted, up a steep hill. We were then given bread to eat, saturated with phosgene. In a further exercise we were subjected to contamination by mustard gas which needed to be hastily wiped away with anti-gas ointment to prevent blisters. After a break for exams, we were then sent on night exercises to be sprayed by moving vehicles throwing out C.A.P. gas. We all found it incredibly exhausting. The next day we had to write up the experience pointing out the dangers.

Worse was to follow. An aircraft sprayed us with G2D, as it was called. This was an imitation mustard gas requiring lengthy decontamination not only of ourselves and our clothing but even of our hair. We had to assume that the service respirators had not been fully protective. Then, after a brief walk to the other side of the camp, we were commanded to decontaminate an entire house in which a 6lb gas bomb was said to have been dropped. This was followed by pulling a "supposed" unconscious colleague out of a ditch and going through the same exhausting decontamination routine.

The following morning came the horrible ordeal of giving our own lectures. Great was my relief when I heard the examiner announce, "That's excellent, you needn't go on, you've obviously got it absolutely taped."

We were packing with the utmost thankfulness when the A.T.S. company commander sent for me.

"I thought you would like to know that the marks have come through. You have been given a 'D'. You are the only 'D' on the course. Congratulations sergeant. Off you go now and enjoy your leave."

'D' stood for distinguished and was much coveted. I felt extremely relieved.

Our Hampshire cottage—Kirklands.   *Plate 7*

It was a very cross-country journey to get to Kirklands but I arrived, late in the evening, almost in the last stage of exhaustion and desperate for a bath. A series of air raids had slowed trains and disrupted traffic in many areas. The little Hampshire cottage was a true haven of peace. There had been a break from air raids for some time and the renewed noise had been disconcerting. The "All clear" sounded at last.

My mother's health had improved a little after a few days with my brother and family, where she had enjoyed a change of scene with the grandchildren. After a week at home, feeling gloriously rested, I accepted Uncle Robert's very kind invitation to his lovely home in Cornwall. My mother's youngest brother, a naval officer in the First World War, he was now very occupied with running a farm. The two young daughters, Averil and Denise were away at boarding school.

Travelling on the night train, I reached Plymouth by early morning. The devastating bomb damage was appalling seen from the train window. With a small amount of petrol, as a result of Home Guard and other duties, Uncle Robert allowed me to travel with him on some of his duties and I much enjoyed the view of the gentle countryside of Cornwall, particularly near the coast with the tang of the sea. The obstructions on the beaches were really formidable with the huge notices "Danger—Keep Clear".

In the family's superbly kept garden, a fresh soft wind seemed to be perpetually blowing from the west. There appeared to be snowdrops, winter aconites, crocuses, grape hyacinths, and primroses all flowering in an exquisite procession. Even a few bluebells were beginning to show in the gorgeous woodlands, surrounding the property. The scenery was very familiar as the property had formerly belonged to our grandfather and my brother and I had spent many happy childhood holidays in this entrancing corner, with its railway station misleadingly named Grampound Road. In those days, it had been a bungalow, built as a shooting lodge, until my uncle, after getting married, had built his own house.

My father kindly met me at Paddington, giving me a delicious meal in his club before I caught the train back to Camberley. The sky gleamed with a rising Easter moon.

CHAPTER TEN

By the summer of 1942 life was becoming much harsher. A great shortage of coal was now menacing. Mines and miners were growing older. Young men had gone into munitions or into the services. The demand for coal for the factories was constantly rising. A new Ministry of Fuel and Power was set up and some young men, known as Bevin Boys, were conscripted to work in the mines instead of joining the armed forces. This was to be the cause of considerable grumbling, bringing some families real distress. But on the whole the national unity remained steady. Most people guessed that, behind the scenes, large numbers of troops were being trained and accumulated for the eventual invasion of France.

C.E.M.A. had been brought into being, Council for the Encouragement of Music and the Arts, and a number of enjoyable concerts were organised in A.T.S. and army units. Only one concert came to Camberley which we shared with the Poles and the Free French.

In June, the Prime Minister was to visit Washington for the second time only to return to the tragic news that Tobruk had fallen. The British army retreated to El Alamein. Now General Rommel had reached his highest point, failing to break through the British lines. To please President Roosevelt, the Prime Minister agreed to an American Supreme Commander in North Africa and the American General Eisenhower was appointed. In August the Prime Minister flew to Cairo and General Sir Bernard Montgomery (later Field Marshal Viscount Montgomery) was given the command of the Eighth Army. He was said to be the best British field-commander since Wellington.

Also in August, we were informed that an *extremely* important person wanted to inspect No. 1 M.T.T.C. and we all set about painting, scrubbing, polishing and making the three requisitioned schools look as spotless as possible. It was a great day for us all when the Queen arrived walking up and down our ranks. Her Majesty lunched with the officers and we were all told later that Princess Elizabeth, then aged sixteen, wanted to join the A.T.S. as soon as she was old enough and that she was hoping to become a driver at Cordwalles. The King had chaffed her that she would never learn the intricacies of the internal combustion engine, and that she would never be able to grapple with tyre changing, and would certainly never grasp map-reading. For once His Majesty was proved entirely wrong! In less than two years the Princess was to become a "student" par excellence.

As the summer ran on I received the summons to be present at an O.C.T.U. board in Reading. My answers to the many questions must have satisfied the board as instructions followed that I was to report to the Officer Cadet Training Unit at Windsor on 1st October, 1942. Three of my fellow sergeants were to accompany me, others had been instructed to report to Edinburgh. I was more than grateful that I had been selected for Windsor as this would enable me to keep in touch with my mother, if and when cadets were given leave. I was now conserving every drop of petrol to be able to continue using my car.

Soon we received news that the Prime Minister had moved from Cairo to Moscow to visit M. Stalin. It was reported that all had gone along with much cordiality and with a hospitality quite forgotten in the hard-pressed United Kingdom. But the Prime Minister spoke cautiously, "We are still in a period of suspense and strain."

The time had now come for me to leave Camberley and I felt quite sad. The commandant sent for me to say "goodbye". "You are leaving us, not with one feather, but with a whole bunch of feathers in your cap, and we are most grateful. Best of luck for your future career as an A.T.S. officer." I thanked her for all her kindness to me with my particular thanks to the adjutant who had given me my chance.

On my last evening in the sergeants' mess I was very touched to be invited to cut a special iced cake with the words "Good luck, Britannia" (my army nickname) written in pink icing sugar. My "F" squad produced a book as a little presentation signed by them all of which I very greatly appreciated. It was certainly quite a wrench to drive away. I felt as if I had been in the A.T.S. other ranks for several years instead of fifteen months.

The Windsor officer cadets were accommodated in yet another boys' school. We were informed that the very young Mr. Rudyard Kipling had spent his earliest school-days in this setting. The O.C.T.U. course of two months consisted of one long rush of lectures, exercises, essays, exam questions, drill, physical training sessions, and much concentrated study of administration. At long last we reached the day of our "Passing Out Parade". I had been appointed "company commander" with the unenviable task of calling out all the commands. My parents nobly attended, and afterwards I was able to accompany them to London where I was granted a few days leave. My dear mother and I shared a room in the Ladies' Carlton Club while my father spent a night or two in his own club and we visited one or two theatres. I was shocked by my mother's frailty, but in her usual unselfish way she made light of it. Later we all drove home to Kirklands where I laid up my car. I had been posted to No. 2 M.T.T.C. at Gresford, which lay between Wrexham and Chester.

At the end of my leave, now attired in an officer's uniform, my father drove me to London. As my mother waved from our little drive, although I did not then realise it, I sensed that I might be seeing her for the last time. I travelled to Chester deeply depressed.

The two months of December and January at the turn of the year 1942-43 were to be the most miserable of all my life. This Motor Transport Training Centre, recently given over to the A.T.S., a former army camp, proved to consist of an immense area of Nissen huts situated in a coal-mining district. There were no pleasant after work amenities as there had been at Camberley. Wrexham was the nearest town but it was a five mile journey, while Chester was nine miles, and the 'bus service was sparse. In addition, I had arrived as the newest second subaltern, a very lowly rank, greatly put upon for the incessant duties of orderly officer, conducting early morning drill, and night duty.

The country was still in double summer-time. Being at the shortest time of daylight, the sun never reached the camp until after 9.00 a.m. accordingly, all our early duties had to be carried out in the black-out with veiled torches. Even torch batteries had now become very hard to discover in the local shops. My work consisted of the boring and repetitive job of copying out by hand the interminable names and army numbers of the driver trainees, together with their rates of pay, which had to be handed to the pay officer at pay parade once a week.

Christmas was brightened by a little holly, but, unlike 1941, in the agreeable environment of Cordwalles, there was only very slight relaxation and no E.N.S.A. company. However, I was happy to feel that my parents had joined my brother and family in their Rickmansworth home where they had spent a happy time. The weather, at least, was kind and there was no snow.

A few days after the New Year of 1943 my brother telephoned with the heart-breaking news that my mother had died. I caught the train from Chester arriving at Euston late at night where he was patiently waiting in the sombre gloom. He and his kind wife gave me sanctuary in their own home until he and I joined my father at Kirklands. I felt quite numb with grief. My mother and I had shared a life-long temperamental sympathy. It had been a relationship of exceptional closeness and harmony, unusual between mother and daughter, and my private mourning was to remain intense for months to come. It had also been a desperate grief to my father and my brother and we were a very stricken family at her graveside in the churchyard of All Saints' Church, Headley, where she was laid to rest. In due course we arranged for a charming gravestone especially designed, with a harpist angel, together with a bird bath, as my mother was a great lover of birds. At a much later date, my brother was to plant a cross of snowdrops with a circle of crocuses, which flourished over her grave.

At my brother's suggestion I applied for a compassionate posting to be nearer my father. I had not expected that anything would result from this, but the A.T.S. showed a human face and by the end of the month I had been posted to London. I was instructed to report to No. 1. M.T. Company R.A.S.C. accommodated in a series of pleasant houses in Cadogan Gardens, Chelsea.

My relief was immense and I was enormously grateful to find that the A.T.S. company commander, Junior Commander E., had been at Camberley. I had not had much to do with her as she had been on the transport side, but she had known me by sight as a lecturing sergeant and was to show me great consideration and kindness. I settled into a one-time gracious Victorian house as her personal assistant in a small and friendly mess of only four officers. We overlooked the pleasant green plane trees of Cadogan Gardens.

CHAPTER ELEVEN

As the sun poured through the attractive windows one clear April morning, the company commander looked up from her desk.

"Britannia I have news for you!" (She had continued with my Camberley name.) "You are to put up your second pip." This was happy news indeed and at lunch time she allowed me an extra half hour to celebrate with my brother, whom I was lucky enough to be able to meet from time to time when our respective lunch-hours coincided. He was still in the Air Ministry but there were to be bigger jobs in front of him.

Thanks to this company commander's exceptional under-standing, for which I was inordinately grateful, I was beginning to come to life again. The war news, too, was much happier. After desperate fighting against the Germans for many months, the Russians had now blunted the German advance. Meanwhile, General Sir Bernard Montgomery had won a brilliant victory at El Alamein and the British and American army under the command of American General Eisenhower had invaded French North Africa. The German General Rommel had been forced to withdraw, leaving immense numbers of Italian and German prisoners. It was said that the British and American leaders were now turning their minds to the invasion of Italy.

The A.B.C.A. pamphlets continued to flow into army units and here I was able to be of some use. I was even lent to other companies to take charge of the discussion groups. About this time great emphasis was being placed on sport in the A.T.S. Tennis and golf clubs generously opened their doors to service members, while bicycling and rambling were also warmly encouraged. Swimming, too, was recommended and I entered a services' swimming competition at the Marshall Street Baths, managing to win the diving shield, to my company's delight.

My father's life was now entering a new phase. He had been

invited to occupy the St. James's Street flat of his friend and publisher, Mr. Walter Hutchinson, with a view to making a start on his book of reminiscences later to be published under the title *Pilgrims and Pioneers.* He therefore finally disposed of the lease of our much-loved former London home, now seriously bomb damaged in Westminster. At the same time he was persuaded to join an Anglo-American Brains Trust enterprise, due to tour service units, a new interest he was to carry out with his own competent skill for the next two years.

My kind company commander had encouraged me to keep in touch with my brother and my father. Occasionally she pushed me out to accompany my father to a theatre no matter how dark the night. One was beginning to get used to poor bomb-tarnished London, with its many boarded-up buildings, and to jump over the rubble and tattered sandbags.

In May I was due for a week's leave. My father pressed me to accept the kind invitation of my mother's elder brother, Sir Samuel Harvey, known in the family circle as Uncle Emile, and his generous wife, Aunt Sybil, for a few days at Dundridge, the once superb Devonshire home of our maternal grandfather, now immensely changed under war-time conditions. In my childhood there had been countless indoor staff and an even greater number of gardeners. Now there remained two gardeners, above call-up age, whose wives gave a little help in the house. My aunt tackled the cooking with help from her daughter, Patsy, a temporary refugee from London with her two little children then aged four and three. Patsy was to return to her Chelsea flat after the war lucky enough to be spared excessive bomb damage. Meanwhile, as we had done in the First World War, the young children were enjoying Dundridge, but in vastly different circumstances.

I was to feel enormous admiration for Patsy after the war, when I was to meet her carrying out the herculean task of scrubbing out her flat, floors, walls and even ceilings to make it habitable for her returning service husband and her little boy and girl. In due course, a younger sister was to join the children.

Uncle Emile was no longer the Member of Parliament for Totnes, a constituency he had represented for many years. He was very busily engaged in Home Guard and many other local affairs, like his younger brother in Cornwall. Evacuees from Plymouth had been looked after at Dundridge, but, in 1943, all had left. My aunt and uncle were proud of their two W.R.N.S. daughters, Pamela and Olivia. Gerry, the youngest was still at school. All were to become very attractive brides within the next years. Aunt Sybil's wish for many grandchildren was to be more than amply fulfilled.

On my return to my army unit in Cadogan Gardens, the company commander greeted me with the news that I was to be "seconded" temporarily to take over the A.T.S. section of 315 M.T. Coy R.A.S.C. in Queen's Gate, Kensington, as acting company commander to replace the junior commander who had fallen ill. I was quite shocked. My understanding of A.T.S. administrative work was minimal.

I was soon to find myself ensconced in Queen's Gate with only a very young newly commissioned second subaltern, even less experienced than I was, to give me a hand. However, we struggled along and I was lucky to find a pleasant major in charge of the whole section who was very helpful. The R.A.S.C. other ranks were occupying a requisitioned hotel in Cromwell Road. This was quite a walk from the A.T.S. headquarters but messages flowed by runners in both directions.

One lovely June morning I received a sudden message from the major, R.A.S.C. asking me if I would combine his other ranks A.B.C.A. discussion with my A.T.S. girls as he had been called away. It was suggested that we should all gather in the Cromwell Road hotel headquarters, where there was more room.

"Thanks very much indeed," he telephoned, "And please choose any subject you like as long as you can get them all talking."

Accordingly, we all shuttled along to the one-time Milton Court Hotel settling ourselves outside in the hotel garden. The great barrage balloons overhead were diamond-clear against the real gentian blue of the morning sky. Ripples of sunlight reached us through the gently quivering leaves of sycamore and lime trees.

"Prediction is a fool's game," I started, "But I thought we might discuss the way you will want to present this war to your grandchildren in forty years time." I had made a good choice. A most animated discussion followed. All I needed to do was prevent the ideas from straying too far from the point. Our allotted hour sped by with considerable enjoyment.

Quite unknown to me, hidden behind hotel curtains, a senior officer from the Army Educational Corps (now Royal Army) was listening with interest. This one discussion group was to have an unexpected influence on my A.T.S. future. At the time I was unaware of anything unusual and proceeded to carry on with normal duties until a new junior commander was posted to 315 Coy R.A.S.C. as the permanent company commander. Joyfully I then returned to Cadogan Gardens, very touched to have received a parting present from the company, a wooden box with all their signatures, made in spare time by one of the recruits. It was a charming thought.

A few days later, after I had carried out the routine house inspection, the company occupied four houses in Cadogan Gardens, my company commander burst out, "Well you certainly have the sparkle of success about you! There is now a request from the Army Educational Corps to enlist you as a junior commander education officer in September and you are requested to appear before a board next month." I was amazed. I had barely heard of the Army Educational Corps, but the promotion to junior commander sounded very exciting.

"I wonder what made them think of me?" I questioned.

"I'll let you into a secret," came the answer. "An extremely favourable report of your record has gone through to the War Office and while you were away I was warned that I might be losing you." She patted my hand. "Well done, my dear. I hope you will go from strength to strength, you deserve it." It was then that I was able to express my gratitude to her which I felt deeply. She had helped me through the most desolate time.

My father and brother were both very pleased with my news. We were able to enjoy a little family dinner in my father's club. There had been extremely tragic news from Aunt Winnie, however, when allied forces had landed in Sicily. One of the many sad casualties had been her son, an only child, Nicholas Ellwood. The news of her boy's death was to cause Aunt Winnie inconsolable grief for a number of years. We all grieved for her. Her sister, Aunt Floss, had now moved to Hampshire, after all her property had been bombed in Birmingham. She was living as a permanent resident in an attractive hotel at Froyle, only a short distance from our cottage, Kirklands. My father was very glad to have her near and they were often in touch. Uncle Bob was still sending most generous food parcels from New Zealand. These were immensely appreciated, and shared round.

The Allied Great Powers were already committed to total victory. The Prime Minister had said at Casablanca at the beginning of the year 1943 at his meeting with President Roosevelt, "We are bound by our consciences to civilisation." But the sands were shifting under British strength and, while the country did not then realise it, leadership was moving to the United States. Great Britain could no longer maintain herself as a great power from her own resources. American strength, meanwhile, was climbing on a massive scale. From their limitless resources the Americans were able to supply a mass of convoy destroyers bringing about a dramatic change in the amount of shipping lost in the Atlantic.

The British "Cupboard" was nearly bare. The public too, were tiring, after having risen to immense heights of sacrifice, heroism and resolution. If the war effort had flagged, and North Africa, Sicily, and Italy seemed far away, very substantial plans were now being worked out to offset the social evils of inequality and want so prevalent before 1914, and, to a lesser extent, before 1939. It was hoped to maintain the high morale.

A new set of pamphlets were being prepared, similar to A.B.C.A. but to be called *The British Way and Purpose.* The work of attempting to educate the service personnel was now to be turned over to a formerly comparatively small service Army Educational Corps which now needed to be enormously increased, mobilising the help of women officers, in order to lay the foundation of reconstruction for after the war. It was into this quite new kind of staff appointment that I was about to be called. I had no means of knowing what was expected of me when I was summoned before a War Office selection board early in August.

CHAPTER TWELVE

In the pearly light of a September morning, looking out of the train window, after many night hours of a bumpy crowded compartment, I saw what can only be described as a veritable symphony of colour: violet sky, pink-tipped drifting clouds, pine coated grape-blue hills, rust-tinted woodlands, thick clumps of purple heather, and white sheep contentedly grazing. It was a scene of dazzling loveliness in remarkable contrast to the drab, shabby, dirty, rubble-encrusted, bomb-scarred streets of London. Someone seemed to have opened a fairy tale jewel box.

I had duly passed the selection board held in Eaton Place, yet another requisitioned house, and was now on my way to Perth having been posted as Staff Officer III with the rank of Junior Commander (Captain). I was to work in South Highland District, part of Scottish Command. It had been something of a shock to hear that my posting was as far as Scotland but I was looking on it as a great challenge.

The train drew into Perth, a delightful town of which I knew nothing, and I was most relieved to find a pleasant A.T.S. subaltern awaiting me. Helping me into the army staff car, she explained, "The A.T.S. officers are living in Balhousie Castle. This is the normal headquarters of the Black Watch Regiment but they have generously handed it over for the duration." Entering the drive I was impressed by this fine imposing building erected in Scottish baronial style. The subaltern continued, "We'll have breakfast first and then I'll take you along to meet Senior Commander T. at head office. She is looking forward to greeting you. You are our first A.T.S. education staff officer. Unfortunately, you may have to live in Dundee. The education staff have just moved from Perth."

The officer in command of the A.T.S. of South Highland District, Senior Commander T., greeted me enthusiastically.

"We are really delighted to have you here," she told me, "But it is unfortunate that your education office should have moved to Dundee". She then explained that my Staff Officer II, Major McK., had arranged for me to be put up in a local hotel.

"He is expecting you this morning so I suggest you catch the next train to Dundee, leave your luggage in the station and then take a taxi to 299 Perth Road."

It was mid-morning by the time I reached the address in Perth Road and climbed the stairs in yet another one-time Victorian house which had obviously seen better days. Knocking on a door marked "S.O. II Education, South Highland District" I found a most breezy, genial, major, with shaggy eyebrows and a marked Scottish accent. He ran towards me grabbing both my hands.

"Welcome, lassie, welcome!" he burst out. I had not expected such agreeable enthusiasm and was most happily surprised. Major McK. continued, "This is my colleague Lieut L.," introducing me to a much younger officer rather hidden behind the door, "And as you know, my name's McK. I can't tell you how pleased we are to have an A.T.S. lassie with us. Lieut. L. has booked a room for you in the Station Hotel. We lunch at Draffens and then L. will help you to get your luggage out of the station."

Draffens proved to be a department store in the centre of

Plate 8

Mr. Churchill at Ramsgate leaving a bombed shop.

Dundee, a long walk from the education office. At lunch the two officers explained that they had moved from Perth because they had had to share unpleasantly cramped quarters with the entertainments officer and the army padré. "We had no room to move," said Major McK., "And then a Dundee house became available. It was grand for us, as we both live in Dundee." I wondered then if the arrangement would prove equally good for me.

My early suspicion was to prove well-founded, but it was to be some time before I was able to make a satisfactory change. Meanwhile, a shock awaited me at the Station Hotel. After my first night the manager approached me, "I believe there has been a misunderstanding, I can only take you up to the week-end. The officer accompanying you yesterday appeared to think that he had made a permanent booking for you. I am very sorry but this is not the case."

Explaining my dilemma to Major McK. on reaching the Perth Road house, he advised me to go straight to the police. "They keep addresses of reputable boarding-houses suitable for service personnel," he informed me. "In fact I will 'phone as it is imperative for you to get accommodation as quickly as possible. Dundee is bursting at the seams."

Before the end of the morning the police telephoned a list of addresses. In my lunch hour, I bought a map of the city streets and endeavoured to track down the addresses provided. All looked terrible, but the least bad appeared to be in Windsor Street where a friendly Mrs. McD. agreed to let me have a room. The good Lieut. L. gave me a hand again with moving my heavy luggage from the Station Hotel. Both he and Major McK. were married men living in their own homes.

The boarding house in Windsor Street was an extraordinary experience. It was not at all comfortable with only one bath and wash basin on the first floor, while I had been relegated to the fourth floor. The living-cum-dining room on the ground floor was extremely congested including a baby in a pram. The poor little baby slept in the pram while her mother appeared to occupy a sofa in the same room. My fellow boarders were three elderly men, two youngish school teachers, both women, and the family who owned the house, parents with two daughters. I had to make the best of it.

CHAPTER THIRTEEN

In this late September of 1943, Dundee seemed mellow and golden beneath a blue haze of sky and I admired the orange and scarlet dahlias glowing in the well-kept gardens on my way to the education office headquarters in Perth Road. Now the time had come for me to accompany Major McK. on his round of the South Highland District Units. He drove his own staff car and these were very enjoyable journeys visiting so many Scottish towns: Dunfermline, Alloa, Kinross, Kirkcaldy, Coupar Angus, Pitlochry, Blairgowrie, Stirling and Dunkeld, to name but a few. It was all enchantingly new to me. I can still recall the luxuriant vividness of the exquisite scenery, the sea at St. Andrews, ultramarine, laced with emerald, the autumn shadows with the sunlight flickering over the shoulder-high michaelmas daisies coloured in every shade of mauve, the lochs like sapphires and the rivers like pale steel. When we set off early there were spiders still on their silken threads riding in the fresh breeze, while a few remaining butterflies danced in and out among the purple asters and late flowering lavender. And soon the earth was to glow red-brown with the falling leaves.

Greatly as I enjoyed myself, however, I realised that my work for the A.T.S. for which I had been posted to Scotland, was non-existent. Obviously I would need to make some move to get back to Perth. If I could live at Balhousie and meet the A.T.S. officers and thus get to know their needs, I thought, I could still travel into Dundee every day.

The Windsor Street boarding house provided breakfast, and a very filling "high tea". The three elderly men were retired civil servants, recalled for the duration. The younger daughter of the house helped her mother with cooking and housework while the older girl worked in the public library. Mr. McD's employment remained a secret, but he was always seated at table when it was meal time. It was a struggle to understand his accent.

Indeed, it was a struggle to come to terms at all with this most unexpected life in a Dundee boarding house, a situation I had never envisaged. With extreme suddenness, however, I received instructions to report to the Army School of Education in Wakefield for a week's course, to be followed by a second week in Warwickshire House, London.

The Wakefield course was most pleasurable. It was here that I was to meet my fellow A.T.S. education officers for the first time, and I also got to know my immediate superior, Senior Commander G., who was at Scottish Command headquarters in Edinburgh. This officer was a charming person admitting to me at once that she had been concerned to hear that I had been obliged to seek accommodation in Dundee so far from the district headquarters. We had an immediate conversation about this.

"I think you should get into the mess at Balhousie as soon as you can," she advised, while I replied that I had had every intention of trying to make this arrangement as soon as I had got to know Major McK. and the actual office work a little better.

We were entertained by many admirable lectures, even amusing ourselves with evening charades. At the end of the week, we all travelled together to London settling into a huge building at the back of Tottenham Court Road. Once again the lectures were excellent and very informative. It was a joy to be able to spend an evening with my father and to telephone my brother. I even managed a visit to my former company commander still in Cadogan Gardens, who showed keen interest in all my news.

By the time the second course ended we were all granted 48 hours leave and I accepted Aunt Winnie's generous invitation to join her in her Sheffield home.

Bravely struggling against the immense grief at the recent loss of her son, Aunt Winnie gave me a wonderfully happy time. We saw two or three cinemas but the bomb damage to the centre of Sheffield was devastating and shocked me considerably. Aunt Winnie had taken on some part-time work in the local hospital. She had a brilliant brain having achieved a double "First" at Girton in the last years of Queen Victoria's reign. Aunt Floss's move to Hampshire had pleased her. "It will be nice for both her and your father to be able to keep in touch," she told me. Immensely eager to get news of my brother and family I was able to tell her that I had been on the telephone very recently and that all seemed to be well.

October was well advanced by the time I found myself back in the education office in Perth Road. Now I took the chance of making the suggestion to Major McK. that I should live in the A.T.S. officers' mess in Perth and travel daily to Dundee. He was upset to begin with, as I had feared he might be.

"But I shan't see nearly as much of you, lassie."

"If I catch the 8.05 train at Perth I can be here before 9.00 a.m. and I will have had the chance of mixing with the A.T.S. officers and finding out what their units need," I persisted. It took a little time, but eventually I talked him round.

Plate 9

My father in Wales, handing a copy of his latest book to his hostess Lewes Cording. The well-known artist had recently presented him with her charming painting of the "Sir Harry Brittain" carnation.

Senior Commander T. at district headquarters welcomed me with enthusiasm. "I said all along that it was ridiculous to make you live in Dundee where you were never likely to get to know any of the A.T.S. units. I have arranged for you to go straight into Balhousie and there is a room waiting for you." I expressed my appreciation and thanks.

At last I was in a position to carry out the educational activities I had so much wanted to set in motion for the South Highland District units.

Now my whole life was to change. If the officers' mess at Balhousie Castle had been a hotel I would certainly have awarded it five stars. Spotlessly clean with delicious meals, unlimited hot water, and the pleasure of sitting round a real fire getting to know my fellow officers in the evenings, provided the most enjoyable experience in my army life. In addition, I had the good luck to find that an old pre-war acquaintance, Major Greville Stevens, held a high position in the district headquarters. Mr. Stevens, as he had been in earlier days, had married an old friend, Miss Betty Hulton, daughter of Sir Edward Hulton, the newspaper magnate, an old colleague of my father. Betty had died in childbirth, leaving her son, Jocelyn Stevens, to become a further power in the newspaper world. Mr. Greville Stevens had remarried in due course, and his second wife turned out to be Junior Commander Stewart Stevens, in command of the local A.T.S. unit. The major and his A.T.S. officer wife were both living in the Station Hotel, Perth.

On learning that I was the new A.T.S. staff officer for education they were kind enough to invite me for meals and both became of enormous help. Looking back, I doubt if I could have managed without their joint support. So now I went ahead with my plans. I organised cookery classes, embroidery and dressmaking sessions, handicraft evenings, lectures on home-making and simple accountancy, quiz competitions, film shows and visits to the local repertory theatre. In all this work I received great help from the civilian authorities and from my own senior officer in Edinburgh.

After about a month I was instructed to undertake lecturing myself to all A.T.S. units on the subject of "The course of the war". I found it all an extremely rewarding experience. In time some excellent reports were to find their way back to Major McK., so he, too, expressed his gratification.

CHAPTER FOURTEEN

Glorious sunsets smouldered in the evening light, two hours behind natural time, as the country was still adhering to double summertime. In the mornings the eastern sky was only just brightening as I made my way towards 299 Perth Road, after a "blacked-out" journey from Balhousie officers' mess.

Major McK., delighted with my work, persisted on my accompanying him on his many tours. This was an immense waste of time for me usually resulting in my having to spend many hours at night and over the weekends working in my bedroom, where I kept my own small typewriter. My fellow officers were sympathetic but there was no alternative.

At the end of November I received instructions to lecture to a company of W.R.N.S. stationed at Rosyth. A special naval car was sent to collect me and I found this an interesting experience. The W.R.N.S. were a very alert and receptive audience and asked many questions. They were envious of some of the courses I was now running for the A.T.S., the officer in charge pressing me for as much information as I could give her. It seemed as if the army far outstripped the navy with other ranks' educational activities at that time.

When we reached December, I persuaded Junior Commander Stewart Stevens, as the senior district officer commanding an A.T.S. company to invite Major McK., so that he could attend one of the homecraft courses which I had now established. He certainly delighted in this and from then on agreed to my spending two whole days on my own in Perth thus freeing me from all the evening work.

"You are doing splendidly, lassie!" he exclaimed. This new arrangement was to help me a great deal.

Winter was now rapidly approaching as 1943 wound to its close. Sicily had been occupied by allied forces since August and the

Italian dictator, Benito Mussolini had resigned. Soon the allies were advancing, but not without great hardship clawing their way up the Italian peninsula.

On the home front, Lord Woolton, the extremely successful Minister of Food had become Minister of Reconstruction. Bomber Command continued with its attack against German industrial centres, the Ruhr, Hamburg and Berlin. The public sensed that future preparations for the second front, the invasion of France, were being carried out in the utmost secrecy. There were to be two more fiendish German inventions to hit the long-suffering public in the near future, the V-1 (dubbed the Doodlebug) a pilotless aircraft which exploded on crashing, causing enormous damage, and the V-2, a rocket, arriving without warning at a terrifying speed and causing even greater damage. To the brave citizens of London, who were to bear the brunt of most of these raids, the onslaught was both physically and psychologically devastating. In due course, the advance of the allied armies in France was to overrun most of these launching sites but not until there had been a sad number of casualties.

Entitled to leave at Christmas, I joined my father at Kirklands. It was to be the first Christmas without my mother and we were both to feel a deep sense of bereavement. Aunt Floss joined us, and happily I was able to persuade her to stay on for a few days over the New Year to be with my father. He was becoming busier with his broadcasts to the U.S.A. and had been allotted a few extra gallons of petrol which had been of great help to him.

During my brief leave I had managed to pay a visit to my brother and family, the two children, now six and four having developed a good deal. My niece had started nursery school. A most engaging child she always seemed the centre of many friends. Her young brother was more of a "loner". Their kind maternal grandmother, who lived in Edinburgh, had most generously invited me for a night on my way back to Perth. I very much appreciated her hospitality and enjoyed being shown round that lovely city. At a much later date, when making another visit to Edinburgh, I was happy to be able to return a little of her kindness.

Now the calendar was to mark 1944; the last of the scuttling leaves appeared to be hurrying to be free of the hoar frost dropping like icing sugar, and there was a sharpness in the air. Looking out

of my bedroom window, once again in the warm comfort of the
A.T.S. officers' mess, the black-out was total but in the star-
studded sky of indigo velvet I could perceive a faint yellow light
where there was a wasted slip of a waning moon. How much longer
was this war to last, we all wondered?

Major Stevens had been kind enough to find me a small office in
the district headquarters for my days in Perth. This had been
allotted to a former personnel selection officer who had moved to
North Highland District. It was a great boon to be able to use an
official army telephone and Major McK. had come to visit me and
had given his approval. Almost before I had settled in, however, I
received instructions to report to St. Andrew's University, then
requisitioned by the War Office, to attend a course on
"Reconstruction after the war". The chief guest speaker was to be
Lord Woolton. This was the first actual course to be held on post-
war rehabilitation with mention of the newly planned "Welfare
State" and we were all most interested.

Unable to stride along the glorious swathe of yellow sand, still
barbed-wired and not yet untrammelled from anti-invasion
obstructions, we took our exercise on the springy turf listening to
the surging and thundering waves of a wind-swept sea lashing
themselves against the shore. At this course I was to meet a most
pleasant Major H. He and I got on well and carried out a number
of noteworthy conversations. In private life he had been a
schoolmaster. He told me a little sadly how much he missed his wife
and two young sons.

"You are not as fortunate as my Major McK.," I told him. "He
manages to get home to his wife in his Dundee home every night,
hence the nuisance of having my education headquarters in a
different town!" I then described my awkward double life, two
days in a borrowed office in Perth and the remaining days touring
from Dundee. "You have no idea how dark it is in the early
mornings travelling to Dundee," I continued. "There is not enough
light to read which is a great deprivation."

"The double summer-time is a great hindrance in the mornings,
but it does help in the evenings," he wound up.

Lord Woolton spoke very well. We all found it a stimulating
experience. I was about to board the train to return to Perth when
my senior officer, Senior Commander G., sent for me.

"Colonel F. from Scottish Command wants to speak to you," she told me. "Don't be worried as I am right behind you, but he is opposed to your office in Perth. He is an old "Regular" very hostile to all A.T.S., and particularly to those who show enterprise and initiative. You are top of the league there! Let him have his say. He feels you should have acted "by the book", never moving from Major McK's side." A few moments later, in the station waiting room, I found myself confronted by Colonel F. Major McK., anxious to get home, had disappeared. Having given his approval he no doubt preferred not to become implicated.

This was my first meeting with Colonel F., although my colleagues had described him as "a bumbling old blatherer". I felt they were "on target" as I listened to the good colonel telling me that it was the job of the A.T.S. Staff Officer III to stay by the side of the Major Staff Officer II, acting as his right hand. Having been advised to let him have his say I made no defence and put up the pretence of agreeing. Obviously he had no knowledge whatever of my particular circumstances. The lecture was to continue in the same strain until, fortunately, the train for Perth drew up to the station platform

"Well, sir," I said, "I do hope I may have the honour of showing you what I have been organising for the units in Perth one day, meanwhile, I am sure you will allow me to board this train, if I miss it, it will be a wait of three hours." A little grudgingly, I thought, he stepped aside, and I shook hands endeavouring to smile politely. In the background unseen by the colonel, my Senior Commander G. gave me the thumbs up signal. All I could do was to hope that the interview had not left me with too black a mark. I could understand that young women officers, full of energetic new ideas, would be an anathema to the elderly "regulars". War was supposed to be a male prerogative.

In the chilly dampness of this winter evening I made my way back to the warm friendliness of Balhousie. I could still feel the wind tearing around me suggestive of the recent song of the sea. We had been told of the forthcoming "Welfare State". "Do you suppose it will be a parasite state?" one of the officers had asked Lord Woolton. There had been no reply.

CHAPTER FIFTEEN

Winter's bare trees were just beginning to bud and the wind seemed gusty and uncertain as March opened and I was sent off to attend another educational course at Harlech. This was held in a college at a seaside rallying point on the coast of Wales where I was happy to make the further acquaintance of new colleagues. Here we slept in dormitories, and, unlike St. Andrew's, were able to plod along the inviting sands free from anti-invasion obstructions and minefields.

War Office lecturers abounded and we were given considerable information about the future rehabilitation plans and the construction of the new welfare state. This was followed by a session of our own personal lectures on any subject chosen by ourselves. I decided on a phrase of the peace-time Prime Minister, Mr. (later Earl) Baldwin. "Life's greatest success is not the good fortune of a perfect set of cards at the outset but making the most of a poor hand." This was most kindly received and I was awarded a "D" mark for the course which was most gratifying.

The audiences for my obligatory lectures in Perth on "The course of the war" appeared to be growing and Major Stevens asked if I would allow him to send in some Black Watch recruits. I enlisted the help of the good Lieut L. from Dundee to draw the maps on a blackboard and Major McK. asked if he could also take part. The latter had spent some of his early life as a schoolmaster and we had some quite lively times.

Towards the end of March, through the auspices of the London-based organisation called C.E.M.A., we were given the information that the distinguished actress, Sybil Thorndike (later Dame Sybil), was to be lent to South Highland District for a week. It was to be my great privilege to organise her tours.

Miss Thorndike was an enchanting companion. In the car, and also in the hotels where I had sought accommodation for her, she gave me the inspiring story of her life, her struggle to be an actress, her marriage to Lewis Casson, her four children, two sons and two daughters, her strong religious background and her hopes for the future. From unit to unit she gave the most inspiring performances saving up the best for the last, her unique two hours to the A.T.S. officers in Balhousie mess. We were all fascinated and immensely stimulated. It was particularly memorable for me as she had known and been very fond of my mother and held great respect for my father. Her non-stop solo recitals must have been utterly exhausting but when I saw her off eventually at Perth station she looked wonderfully fresh. She must then have been approaching the later sixties. I sent an enthusiastic thank-you letter to the director of C.E.M.A.

On returning from Inverness, a day or two later, where I had been on a joint conference with my northern colleagues, Senior Commander G. from Scottish Command, telephoned to let me know that she and Colonel F. would be making a visit to Perth that week. I arranged to show them, as best I could, the work I had been carrying out for the A.T.S. units. At the end of their visit I had made plans for them to lunch at the Station Hotel. By chance Major Stevens with his attractive wife were also lunching. Asking if they might join our table, both proceeded to praise my job as education staff officer very highly, much more than I deserved.

At Perth station, Colonel F. generously admitted that he had made a mistake when he had chided me at St. Andrew's for what he had assumed to be an impertinence in moving to Perth away from my Dundee headquarters. "I am very much impressed," he maintained. "Quite obviously you took the right course and I warmly congratulate you. I am sorry to tell you now that South Highland District is to be merged with Lothian and Border soon after Easter. I think you will be wanted in Anti-Aircraft Command."

Easter was now very near, and the disclosure of the imminent ending of South Highland District caused us some concern. We were all sad and I had barely time to thank the civilian authorities who had been so helpful, before I was to receive my posting instructions to report to 4th Anti-Aircraft Group Headquarters in Chester at the end of April. I was granted a week's leave before undertaking the new appointment.

Before departing I received a charming letter from Senior

Commander G., who wrote, "I'm extremely grateful to you for the superb job you have carried out in Scottish Command in such a short time. I have never known anyone win goodwill so quickly and so widely. It has also been such fun to work with you, I have so much admired your bubbling enthusiasm and your sense of humour. Very good luck for your new job. I hope we shall be able to keep in touch. Unfortunately I have to enter a nursing home for an operation so I may not be around for a little time." It was a grief that I was never to see this most pleasant person again. The operation failed and she died at the tragically early age of thirty-five.

My fellow officers saw me off at the station presenting me with a delightful book inscribed with all their names. I set off on my journey south with a real sense of loss.

At Kirklands where my father was waiting to greet me I was faced with an unpleasant surprise. A young woman called L. had been established as a living-in secretary to help my father with the book which his publisher, Mr. Walter Hutchinson, had urged him to write. L. was apparently a brilliant stenographer but suffered from a mental disability which caused her to have what my father referred to as "turns" at unexpected times. Instantly my arrival brought on a "turn" and I was horrified. As my father's need of a stenographer, at that moment, was obviously urgent, I decided to withdraw and to spend my leave at my London club. In London the V-1s, or "Doodlebugs" as the newspapers were calling them, were at their height. Two had already fallen in the closely packed Hyde Park area near St. George's Hospital; and in the small hours another fell in Grosvenor Place shattering my bedroom windows and showering the whole room with glass. Not feeling too brave I took refuge under the bed, thankful that I had taken the precaution of putting all my clothes, shoes included, into a wardrobe. At least I would not have to climb into glass splinters when the morning came.

The remainder of the night seemed very noisy, much of it caused by our own A.A. batteries, but wrapped in an eiderdown, and with a makeshift mattress, I managed a very brief sleep. When morning arrived the little maid, whom I had known at the Ladies' Carlton ever since my mother had made me a present of membership in my débutante days, knocked on the door and brought in a breakfast tray. "Your breakfast, madam," she announced, handing me the tea, toast and marmalade without raising an eyebrow at my unexpected position under the bed. "Well, what sort of a night did you have, Letty?" I asked her. "Pretty fair, madam," she replied. "We are all living-in now and getting what rest we can in the old kitchens. I think the members are worse off than the staff." She then went on in the most matter-of-fact sort of way, "I'll get the hoover to rid you of some of this glass."

Plate 10

A poster urging volunteers to "Join the A.T.S.".

That day I was happy to be able to lunch with my brother at the Bath Club, just returned from a mission in the Mediterranean. While most people guessed that invasion of Northern France was probably imminent, preparations remained a most guarded secret to all except those closely involved.

"To the ordinary public there still seems to be no end to this wretched war," I said to my brother, as we walked together in St. James's Park among the halo of cherry blossom, white-pearled narcissi, suntipped daffodils and scarlet tulips. It was delightful to be able to enjoy a few minutes of the peace of the lake, the enchanting bird life, and the scent of early lilac. This was the scene of our very young childhood years, but at that time 1915-16 the water in the lake had been drained. On this occasion it was the sandbagged trenches which had brought about so much unsightly disfigurement.

My brother gave me a little of the London war news. It appeared that General Charles de Gaulle had now made himself the sole leader of resurgent France. De Gaulle was thought to be a very prickly ally with the Prime Minister commenting, "I have borne many crosses in my time, but none so heavy as the Cross of Lorraine!" I also heard that the ban on the ringing of church bells to signify German invasion was about to be removed.

Air raid shelters had been much improved since 1939. The Ministry of Health and the Red Cross had raised the standard of comfort and hygiene as far as could be expected in such squalid circumstances.

I told my brother of my new posting to 4th A.A. Group, Chester, confessing that I had been upset at the thought of travelling again to Chester, so fraught with the horrible memory of the Motor Transport Training Centre at Gresford and the heartbroken journey I had made from Chester after receiving his news of our mother's death. "Well, don't forget there is a huge difference between a second subaltern and a junior commander staff officer," he reassured me, "And you will probably find the new job just as challenging as the one you have left in Scotland." Eventually, he gave me a hand with my luggage as the train left Euston.

CHAPTER SIXTEEN

As my brother had rightly surmised, the next eighteen months were to prove an enthralling experience. The headquarters of 4th Anti-Aircraft Group, where I reported at the end of April 1944, was stationed on the outskirts of Chester in a house called "The Firs". The very large grounds were filled with the now familiar Nissen huts spread out in an enormous circumference to accommodate the staff. The A.T.S. personnel selection officer who had kindly met me at Chester station escorted me to the education offices to meet my Major Staff Officer II, and I was absolutely delighted to find it was the same Major H. whom I had met and liked so much at St. Andrew's. He greeted me very warmly. "I have only been here a month myself," he told me, "And I can't tell you how pleased I was to hear that you were to join me as the S.O. III for the A.T.S." He and I were to work together in close harmony for many happy months and I could not have been luckier.

But the accommodation, particularly after the exceptional comfort of Balhousie, was deplorable. I was shown into a dark, dirty house with the name of "Allenby" which looked as if it had not been swept for weeks. Officers were obliged to share, which I had not experienced since Gresford, and the actual joint mess and dining-room were situated inside the headquarters area, a long walk away, particularly on wet mornings.

It turned out that the general officer in command, Major General B., was away on tour so I was not called upon to meet him for a few days. He had the reputation of being something of an ogre and was thought to be a somewhat ruthless commanding officer.

The area of this group was immense, covering the whole of Wales and including the important towns of Liverpool, Manchester and Birmingham.

It took quite a little time to become familiar with the command organisation of groups, brigades, regiments and batteries. The area also included Anglesey and the Lake District, together with Preston, Lancaster and right up to Carlisle. The best way of travelling to Cardiff and then up to Carlisle would have been a helicopter. As it was, one was lucky to be allowed an army car for special occasions; otherwise one travelled by train. Some of these journeys, where the train connections were poor, often took many hours, and I was grateful to the kind volunteers from the Women's Voluntary Service who manned the trolleys, pushing the more-than-welcome coffee and sandwiches.

After about ten days, the G.O.C., Major General B., returned to headquarters and I was informed by the military secretary that, as a new officer, he wished to meet me. "Be careful, he will eat you from the feet up if you displease him," chaffed my colleagues. Thus warned, I knocked gently on the general's door and was agreeably surprised to find a most genial personality not at all overbearing and possessed of an explosive sense of humour. After one or two questions about my former educational activities in South Highland District, he asked what I thought about the Army Educational Corps in general. Much encouraged by his friendliness I opened out a little, even venturing to describe my contretemps with the 'bumbling old blatherer' from Scottish Command, although naturally omitting that phrase. He laughed heartily and then queried, "Did you say your name was Brittain? Are you by any chance a relation of Sir Harry Brittain?" On my answering "I am a daughter, Sir," he flung back his head with a loud chortle. "Well, isn't that interesting? Your father and I were fellow gold staff officers together at the 1937 Coronation Ceremony in Westminster Abbey. Your father had had a row with the Duke of Norfolk and had been demoted to Block 'Z'! He and I shared a bottle of wine during the proceedings!"

"The Duke of Norfolk was extremely difficult," the general continued, "But what was the actual row about?" Very briefly I explained how my father had wanted to get the press into good seats, and the duke, detesting the press, had demurred. "Well, I would love to meet your father again," pursued the general. "Isn't he due in Chester shortly to take part in the Anglo-American Brains Trust Tour?" I replied that this was the case. "Then, make sure that you tell my A.D.C. and I will get him to dine with me.

Meanwhile, I am very pleased to have you on my staff."

Back in the education office a short time later my colleagues questioned, "Did he cut you into little pieces?" "He was conviviality personified," I replied, but I kept the unexpected social contact to myself.

Meanwhile, I was utterly disgusted with "Allenby", and, at Major H's suggestion, asked the A.T.S. chief commander if I could have permission to go into billets. She agreed readily, explaining that she herself had disliked "Allenby" but that when 4th A.A. Group had moved from Preston, there was no other big enough house available so they had had to make the best of it.

The camp commandant gave me some addresses of local houses who had volunteered to put up army officers for the duration. "Some are pleased to do it," the camp commandant confided, "You see, you only sleep there, all your meals are naturally in the mess, and the householders get quite well paid." Thanking him I looked through the addresses and chanced on one house called "Gartmore", a place in Scotland, where I had lectured to the A.T.S. Perhaps that name might be a lucky omen, I thought, so I rang the doorbell and waited. It proved to be a most happy choice, the owners, a Mr. and Mrs. V., were soon to become the kindest of friends.

CHAPTER SEVENTEEN

The warm loveliness of May, with the rich colours of rhododendron bushes, horse-chestnut trees in full flower, beguiling bird-song, and the quavering cuckoo, proclaimed that the high tide of summer was drawing near. I had now toured widely in this extensive Group area. It had struck me that while the charming city of Chester seemed anchored to the Middle Ages, with England's roots locked in the past, the city of Birmingham appeared symbolic of the industrial age. It was in Birmingham that I now needed to devote my next few days.

Having visited the officers of 34 Brigade with their relevant regiments and batteries, I was escorted to the Group School of Education called Chadwick Manor. This was a delightful house, a former very up-to-date golf club and annexe in beautiful country surroundings, slightly south of the great Midland city. Here there were courses taking place on all kinds of subjects, music, literature, art, many discussions on the "British Way and Purpose" and, of course, lively A.B.C.A. sessions. A number of civilian instructors had been lent from the Workers' Educational Association, many of whom were unashamedly Socialist. It was the first time that I had seen the powerful influences at work bearing down on the men and women of the services which might well produce far-reaching changes in the aftermath of the war.

Back in Chester, Mr. and Mrs. V., who were to give me the sanctuary of their home for many months, treating me like a daughter, showed much interest in my work. I was to owe them both a debt of gratitude. Meanwhile my complaints about "Allenby" had been effective with the house undergoing improvements. My fellow A.T.S. officers were very appreciative. "We had all put up with it like sheep" they told me. Carefully I refrained from making the reply, "Well, more fools you!"

Early in June, the Anglo-American Brains Trust Tour, in which my father was participating arrived in Chester. They were to entertain units in Western Command which were quite separate from the units in the 4th A.A. Group area. My father invited me to dinner at the Grosvenor Hotel to meet the members of the Brains Trust which was most enjoyable. The following night having been invited by the general, the A.D.C. came to collect us both to a pleasant house called Upton Heyes where the general was billeted. This proved to be a most memorable evening.

My father was very taken by the general, a man of most outstanding ability and culture. He had served in the First World War, being awarded the M.C. and had also been in command of the Fortress of Malta's artillery during the siege of 1942. It was said that his wonderful spirit had transformed the whole backbone of the gunners who had been left to bear the brunt of the enemy attack.

The A.D.C. too, a most charming man, Captain R., turned out to be an old friend who had met my father before the war at a shoot belonging to Lord Greenway in a house named Stanbridge Earls, later a boys' school.

The evening was a turning point for me. It was to be the first of many occasions when I was to have the privilege of a purely social contact with the general. He and my father talked most animatedly, laughing delightedly at their joint recollection of the Coronation Day in 1937 when they had first met.

"If you could find time," my father suggested to the general, "I would be very happy to entertain you in our Hampshire cottage. I don't know if you can find some excuse to bring you to the southern end of the country." "I would like that very much," the general replied, an assignation that was to take place in due course.

Once again, another lucky coin had dropped into my "plate". It had happened with the adjutant at Camberley, Major Greville Stevens in Perth, and now in Chester, with the link that my father and the G.O.C. had met in the Coronation Ceremony before the war. Some good fairy certainly seemed to be holding my hand and I felt very grateful. From now on, life appeared to take wings.

Major H. and I were perpetually on the move. I had arranged a homemaking course for the A.T.S. in Coventry which we went to visit, followed by his drama course in Cardiff. Then came a handicraft exhibition in Liverpool in which we had both taken part, together with long discussions in Liverpool University with the heads of what were then called "Regional Commissioners" admirable people who helped us greatly with our work for the forces. Similar talks followed in Birmingham, Manchester and Cardiff. Finally, we returned to Preston to attend a week's course at Cuerden Hall the official Army School of Education for the northern area.

Meanwhile, during our absence from group headquarters, the long-awaited Second Front had started with the Normandy Campaign. The landing operation was thought to be the most formidable ever undertaken in war. "D-Day" has been so fully described in books, films, television and sound radio that it has now passed into history. The great Allied advance, although faced with bitterly stubborn resistance for many months, was to lead to eventual victory and to the ending of the war in Europe. It was no easy walk-over, however, but a fierce struggle with many casualties. As the year drew on, the Russians in the east were also able to take up the offensive. And now I received news that my brother had been sent on a delicate mission to the U.S.A.

A chance engagement had given the general the opportunity of spending a night with my father at Kirklands. Our dear French cook had apparently excelled herself, despite the acute civilian rationing, and my father's cellar, so I was informed later, had reached the peak of hospitality! To express his appreciation, the general presented his host with a most charming seventeenth century portrait of a Sir Harry Brittayne, which had proved an enormous success.

Meanwhile, Major H. and I were working hard in the Birmingham area where there were to be a number of regimental plays. With some difficulty we had procured shields to present to the winners. The best performance was very spirited, an excellent production of Bernard Shaw's *Androcles and the Lion*. The general had given his consent to be present and handed over the shield with a charming speech. Afterwards he suggested that Major H. and I should both dine with him at the Queen's Hotel where we had a wonderfully entertaining evening.

It was now mid-summer and the weather had turned very hot. After a further tour in the Manchester area I was due for 48 hours leave. Aunt Winnie had most kindly invited me. All my civilian clothes were at Kirklands with the exception of a housework overall which I had found useful for various cleaning jobs to protect my uniform. Aunt Winnie's small garden was cleverly concealed from the road and also from her neighbours, so she allowed me to sit in the overall in order to keep cool. Despite her tragedy over the loss of her son, she kept up her spirits most bravely and eagerly sought news of all the family. Uncle Bob had sent her some delightful photographs from New Zealand, together with a food parcel.

The August clouds changed pattern against the sun, flinging gracious shadows over the glowing harvest hues and ripening blackberries. A course entitled "Music and the Arts" was due to take place in a requisitioned girls' school in Berkshire. I had been selected to attend, the only representative from the Group as there had been few places available. It was to prove immensely enjoyable with orchestral music, picture exhibitions, lectures on sculpture and a number of amusing one-act plays. Then we, ourselves, had to lecture. I had taken another saying of Earl Baldwin's as my subject, "Good luck brings merit, but merit does not always bring good luck." Unknown to me, General B. had arrived to hear the end of this course, listening with interest to our contribution.

I had intended to return to Chester by train, but gladly accepted the general's kind offer of a lift.

"We are off duty," the general told me, "My driver can't hear a sound through the sound-proof partition, so let's regard ourselves as civilians." It was the first of many extremely confidential conversations that I was to be lucky enough to hold with him and he was entrancing company.

"I did enjoy my night with your father," he told me once again. "What a remarkable chap he is! And, by the way, I heard your talk on 'merit'. I thought it most outstanding. You ought to take up politics after the war." He related much about his own life and events in Malta. I was soon to discover that he himself was interested in politics, indeed his interests were extremely widespread including music and literature.

"It would be splendid if we could manage a course on 'Music and the Arts' at Chadwick Manor," I enthused. "Perhaps we might pull it off."

CHAPTER EIGHTEEN

The British and American forces had now begun a vast sweep through France. Daring parachutists were being dropped to seize bridges over the Rhine and lack of communication had divided the German armies. The prospect of German invasion was no longer considered feasible, and while the bitter war in the Far East still had to be fought and won, a Release Scheme with early post-war plans was about to be circulated.

In the meantime I wanted to concentrate on the "homecraft" courses for the A.T.S. units. This was to involve considerable touring around the Group on my own while Major H. concentrated on a "Pursuits of Peace" exhibition. An enthusiastic A.T.S. senior commander, who was to remain a very kind friend for many years after the war, gave me great assistance. In charge of the Cardiff A.T.S. in a house with the gloriously inappropriate name of Valhalla, she put several rooms at my disposal, and this enabled me to pull in civilian instructors and to run a whole series of most worthwhile post-war rehabilitation sessions which were to become extremely popular.

Soon a Miss Hilton, the energetic civilian secretary of the Women's Employment Federation, had been good enough to offer help to the women's services and I was able to persuade her to give an address to all senior A.T.S. officers. There was now talk of the disbandment of certain anti-aircraft batteries whose wartime job was now thought to be redundant. In addition to these, several girls from former balloon barrage and searchlight establishments had also become surplus. For these people, boredom had to be relieved and we stepped up our work with lectures, film shows, basket work, sewing and embroidery, even, where we could find instructors, painting and cookery classes. The organisation was hard work, falling to me personally.

The blue misty smoke from autumn bonfires, yellow cloudscape and lengthening shadows became a reminder that autumn was approaching, together with my leave. As the unpredictable young woman L. had not yet rejoined my father at Kirklands for the commencement of his next book, I travelled south with the intention of spending a few happy days in the cottage in Hampshire where Aunt Floss had been temporary hostess.

Looking out of the train window as we sped past the green yellow and brown patchwork of fields, with the cloud shadows sweeping over rust-tipped trees and church spires looming out of grassy villages I admired the slate-tiled roofs and low stone walls. An American officer seated opposite appeared to sense my thoughts.

"Yeah!" he exclaimed. "That looks mighty good to me, mighty good, the England worth fighting for. You folks certainly put up one hell-of-a-good-show in 1940." A smile may have spread across my face as I answered gratefully, "Your President agreed to Lease-Lend. We would have been sunk without it." At once came the rejoinder, "You English never take credit. You sure are the most refreshing people!" The train spun on.

Aunt Floss had been kind enough to loan me a few clothing coupons which I later returned. These enabled me to buy a dress ensuring me a place at a dinner given by some wonderfully kind friends at the Savoy. Later we all went on to see the amusing comedy *The Man who came to Dinner,* a golden evening, reminiscent of happier pre-war days.

London remained desperately shabby but some of the black-out regulations had been relaxed and flowers were flourishing out of the shattered remnants of one-time buildings, while leaves drifted around, yellow, bronze and crimson.

In November, fulfilling an invitation from General B., my father returned to Chester to give a talk to the 4th A.A. Group Headquarters on the subject of "Liaison with the U.S.A." This time he was the general's guest at Upton Heyes. The G.O.C. escorted him into the mess where, in due course, he was to find himself surrounded by the many good-looking A.T.S. officers who formed part of the headquarters staff. Chaffingly the general drew me aside, "Your father's cut me out. None of my lady officers will look at me now!"

There was soon to be a new phase for all army educational staff which was to become known as "The Release Period". Major H.

and I were summoned to two conferences, one at Harlech which was always a delightful seaside holiday, and the second at Cuerden Hall in Preston. We then needed to speed across Wales to Cardiff for a special handicraft exhibition which was to be opened by the Lord Mayor of Cardiff. We then hurtled back to the Liverpool Co-operative Stores where we had arranged another "Peacetime Pursuits" exhibition. I had also received instructions to restart my lectures, formerly entitled "The course of the war" under the new title of "Rebuilding for peace".

Plate 11

A view of the Ladies' Carlton Club Swimming Bath shortly to be destroyed by German bombs—Author on diving board.

Major H. and I had little time to ourselves but now and again we had an hour or two to spare to admire the town halls, built with the solemn classic grandeur of Victorian style in the later part of the earlier century. We were to become familiar, too, with the imposing hotels, the Midland in Manchester, the Adelphi in Liverpool, and Queen's in Birmingham. We were also enjoying Chadwick Manor, where, by chance, it had turned out that the pleasant colonel in charge was a second cousin of my father. This led to a very happy link for me personally.

As winter drew near, I was sent to the Group Gunnery School in Anglesey, Tycroes, known as the Gunnery Practice Camp. Here I had to lecture to all the A.T.S. other ranks, known as auxiliaries, on the subject of "The Release Period". These Nissen huts were on a cliff-edge, cold, bleak and bare, overlooking a lashing steel-grey sea, while the wind tore around in bursts of fury. The A.T.S. officer in charge seemed absolutely delighted to see me.

"You can't imagine how cut off we feel here," she told me, "It is wonderful to hear news of the outside world and your lecture was superbly stimulating." She was kindness itself bringing me extra blankets and even a steaming mug of cocoa as a "nightcap".

In mid-December, the general's endearing A.D.C. Captain R., whom I had now got to know well, invited me to spend my 48 hours leave with him in his delightful house near Cirencester to meet his wife and pleasant family. He was retiring from the post and the position of A.D.C. was shortly to be taken up by the general's attractive elder daughter who was an A.T.S. subaltern.

Soon the Christmas celebrations were underway. My brother, now back from America, had arranged to take his wife and family to Kirklands to be with my father, a happy plan, which the children afterwards proclaimed that they had enjoyed enormously. In 4th A.A. Group headquarters we spent the traditional army Christmas looking after the troops. In those days television was in abeyance but the radio put on good entertainment. We also organised sing-songs and a fancy-dress dance. On Boxing Day a splendid E.N.S.A. company arrived to give a most spirited performance of *Passing Brompton Road*. A little snow fell and the frost was beginning to cling to the bare trees. Out hearts felt lighter although months were still to pass before victory. Allied unity had stirred hopes throughout Europe.

CHAPTER NINETEEN

Major H. and I had now put in much hard work to bring about a music course at Chadwick Manor. As the year 1945 opened, the gifted Dame Myra Hess came to play, together with a lively orchestra which had been recommended by Sir Adrian Boult. In addition I had inveigled a very dear friend, M.P. for one of the Birmingham constituencies, Sir Patrick Hannon, to give a talk on "My lifetime in Parliament". This course was most enthusiastically received, and the G.O.C. having expressed a strong wish to be present, said to us afterwards, "I do congratulate you people on the work you are doing. I would have given the earth for a course of this sort when I was a young soldier. No one ever gave the slightest consideration to the development of our minds, only to making us physical zombies."

With the imminent disbandment of so many units, handicraft work as an occupation was greatly in demand. Accordingly we had arranged another exhibition in Cardiff to be displayed at the David Morgan Stores. This coincided with a singing competition organised by 45 Brigade at the Reardon Smith Lecture Theatre. The mini-Eisteddfod had been magnanimously backed by Sir Robert Webber of the *Western Morning News*, an old colleague of my father. Dr. Teasdale Griffiths, a genial Welsh musician had been talked into judging the singing, which was to reach a surprisingly high standard. It also happened that a lunch in honour of Sir Robert Webber was due to take place in the Park Hotel the following day.

My father had been invited to speak at the lunch and was the guest of his old friends Mr. and Mrs. Cording for the night. After the competition, Cardiff University generously entertained us all. For the first time since 1939, fairy lanterns lit up the entrances.

With so much work to complete at group headquarters, Major H. and I sped back to Chester, but the general remained to be present at Sir Robert Webber's luncheon celebration.

"Your father was in terrific form," he told me a few days later, "And I have invited him to take part in a Brains Trust session at Chadwick Manor together with Sir Patrick Hannon and a senior officer from Anti-Aircraft Command. Would you make the arrangements?" I replied that I would do so with pleasure, adding that, as many senior officers from group headquarters would probably wish to attend, we would commandeer rooms in the Birmingham Queen's Hotel the night before Sir Adrian Boult's special concert for the services, and in that way attend both functions.

The meeting at Chadwick Manor was to prove a brilliant success with my father's cousin, Colonel S., acting as superb host, and the addition of General Benoy from A.A. Command to join the Brains Trust. My father, always susceptible to pretty girls, got on famously with the general's A.D.C. daughter. We all dined at Chadwick Manor, returning to the Queen's Hotel later, greatly enjoying Sir Adrian's special concert in the city hall the following afternoon. We were then entertained by the pleasant staff of 34 Brigade with a series of joyful madrigals.

Gathering to leave Birmingham the following morning, we found it was snowing heavily. After seeing off my father and General Benoy in a slendid looking army staff car, clanking with snow-chains, our General B. offered Major H. and myself a lift back to Chester in a similar car also rattling and hammering with chains clamped to the wheels. "What a very diverting two days!" announced the general as we arrived safely. "Thank you both for all your hard work, I really appreciate it."

In all the many private talks that I was privileged to hold with the general, during my eighteen months on his staff, he was never to ask questions about colleagues. Indeed, the moment he was off duty, the affairs of the 4th A.A. Group vanished. In his personal life he was a deeply troubled man. Innumerable worries bore down on him, his elderly parents, in their late eighties at that time, his wife's frail health, his only son's loss of a leg in the Middle East campaign, and the future of his two young daughters. Most disturbing of all was, of course, his own future, as retirement from army life drew nearer. My father had given him a number of introductions to prominent personalities, but, in the end, sadly, it was his own poor health and failing eyesight that stood between him and any worthwhile post-war appointment. At the beginning of 1945, however, this was not apparent, and he continued to speculate.

On a journey to Manchester, with Major H. sitting with the driver, the general invited me, once again, to sit beside him.

"Your father has most kindly invited me to London," he told me, "To meet Lord Woolton with a view to a possible future post. I am most grateful to him." He chatted on, adding many confidences which made me remember one of my dear Cornish grandfather's expressions, "If you get involved in confidences, keep them intensely secret, some folk say more than their prayers!" This general was obviously a man who needed to talk.

In Manchester we attended the opening of a house called Holly Royde, newly established as a Release Scheme Education Centre. Disbanding searchlight regiments were now pouring into old Gunsites and there was much agitated discussion as to how they were to be usefully occupied. They were to be labelled by the ridiculous name of "Umbrella Companies".

Plate 12

H.M.
The King
visiting
Kent after
an air
raid.

CHAPTER TWENTY

The winter-flowering heather looked very beautiful outside "The Firs" as I returned from Carlisle after giving yet another series of talks to the A.T.S. auxiliaries on the "Release Scheme". The wind was icy and I was feeling rather unwell having caught a cold, which, as it invariably did, had found its way to my chest. I decided to visit the medical officer.

The medical officer took my temperature. "You are completely worn out, my dear girl," she announced, "Added to which you have developed a slight touch of pleurisy. I am going to send you to Mollington Reception Centre where I want you to stay in bed for a week and then we'll see how you are."

The week in bed was to prove absolute bliss. The snow had reappeared as I lay warm and snug, wearing a delightful pink knitted bed-jacket, given by some kind soul as her contribution to "Comforts for the Troops", and revelling in a glowing coal fire an exceptional luxury. I was even given a boiled egg with real butter on my toast "fingers", almost unobtainable in 1945.

In due course, the medical officer's report found its way to the military secretary's desk who passed it on to the general. Quite concerned, the general and his daughter came to visit me.

"I think you need a rest," said the general. "As soon as you are fit to travel go home on leave." My father rose to the occasion even suggesting that U. (the A.D.C. daughter), might be allowed to accompany me for the weekend, as he had been very taken with her. Permission granted, we both travelled together to Kirklands. Before returning, my father gave us a delicious lunch at the Carlton Club Ladies' Section, and my brother broke away from duty to entertain us very generously at the Bath Club. Despite strict rationing, London clubs retained a high standard.

Back at work again, Major H. and I were now sent off on yet another course. This was to take place at Theobald's Park, a house at Waltham Cross known as "A.A. Command Staff Duties School". The colonel in charge sent for me soon after our arrival greeting me with the words, "I understand you have considerable inventive genius. Will you help us over these 'Umbrella Companies'?" It seemed that the displaced searchlight units, together with disbanding batteries were causing worry. The personnel regarded their contribution to the war as over and were clamouring for release.

In due course, and with considerable help from the civilian authorities, we were able to establish a whole number of well-received activities in the Liverpool and Manchester areas.

At the beginning of March, the news that we had all been told to expect, became official: the closure of 4th A.A. Group and its amalgamation with 5th A.A. Group outside Nottingham. General G. from 5th Group was to retire to be replaced by our General B. As our G.O.C. was a man of formidable personality he succeeded in obliging the military powers to allow him to take at least twenty of his own staff officers with him. I was happy to be destined to accompany them. We were not too popular to begin with, but, in time, we appeared to shake down fairly well.

Before leaving, I was able to entertain Mr. and Mrs V., the extremely kind couple who had taken me into their home, giving them dinner at the Grosvenor Hotel and inviting them to choose a picture for themselves as a mark of my great appreciation. "I shall always be in your debt," I told them as I said "goodbye". "We shall miss you greatly," they kindly replied. It was quite a sad moment as the utility van rumbled me away from Chester on its way towards Nottingham.

The headquarters of 5th A.A. Group had been established in a school in a village called Kimberley, about five miles north-west of Nottingham. This was a mining area and I was not surprised on hearing that I had been billeted in a miner's cottage. My utility van drove me up to a strange little patch of council houses where a most obliging host carried my luggage to the spare room. The only family appeared to be a little boy of about six. This couple were friendly and kind, offering me unlimited baths, a great treat, and wheeling my bicycle into their conservatory.

Happily Major H. and I had not displaced our predecessors so there was no animosity towards us. We settled again in the

Plate 13
H.M. The Queen visiting an A.T.S. field kitchen.

unavoidable wartime Nissen hut as our Education Group headquarters. Early March remained very cold but the days were lengthening and life was in the air with a million tightly-folded buds straining to unfurl.

As the weeks advanced the allied troops began to reach the fringe of Berlin. It was now thought that the end of the war in Europe could not be far. I had been sent on a mission to London with permission to spend the weekend at Kirklands. My father had invited the general to join us on the Sunday, which he did, after having spent a few days in search of a possible appointment connected with the Channel Islands. We spent a delightful day. My father congratulated him on his newly-won C.B.E. Seeing him off at Farnham station he confided, "I have put your name in for the honours list but don't be disappointed if nothing happens, only a very small number are likely to go to A.A. command." I was able to express my genuine gratitude. My kind friend, the senior commander from "Valhalla" received the A.T.S. honour and I was delighted.

I had now been informed that my work for the Army Educational Release scheme would entitle me to a small petrol allowance so I got my small Ford car on the road again. It was thus possible to drive back to Kimberley, stopping the night at my old (co-educational) school in Harpenden where the headmaster and his wife had most kindly invited me. The headmaster, my former fifth form master, at the latter end of the 1920's, told me, very flatteringly, "You were one of my best essay writers, and the rising star of our newly-formed Debating Society. I do hope you will take up public life when the war is over."

After a long drive, I found myself at 5th A.A. group headquarters once again. Major H. and I now needed to visit brigades as far apart as Lowestoft and Newcastle-upon-Tyne. We also commanded activities in a number of busy cities including Norwich, Leicester, Derby, Leeds, Sheffield and Hull. We seemed to be forever travelling but I was grateful for the chance of visiting so many new areas, formerly quite unknown.

In mid-April the country received the news that the American and British forces had crossed the Rhine and penetrated into the Ruhr. At the same time we learned of the much lamented death of President Roosevelt. The former Italian dictator, Mussolini, together with his mistress, had been shot by communists, left ignominiously hanging upside down. The war news was extremely encouraging leading to the belief that the enemy were now doomed.

Hitler, in his Berlin bunker, deeply shocked at Mussolini's insulting death, married his "wife of one day" leaving instructions that both bodies were to be destroyed in a funeral pyre. A day later, Germany accepted unconditional surrender to the allied forces. The Day of Destiny had arrived; the Hitler tyranny was over.

CHAPTER TWENTY-ONE

On 8th May, 1945, V.E. Day (Victory in Europe) was declared with the Prime Minister and the Royal family being acclaimed on the balcony of Buckingham Palace. Church bells rang, flags flew from every building, floodlighting appeared miraculously in the long blacked-out streets, and there was shouting, cheering and madly dancing crowds. But the Japanese war had still to be won and possibly the rejoicing was more temperate than the ecstatic scenes of 11th November, 1918 which I could just recall. Thanksgiving services were now to be held in churches throughout the world.

We ourselves were granted a two-day holiday. No plans had been made to meet this celebration so we enjoyed a dance and a splendid bonfire. The D'Oyly Carte Opera Company were performing *The Mikado* in a Nottingham theatre which many of us flooded in to enjoy before attending the dance. On the second day of the holiday C.E.M.A. produced an excellent concert at the Albert Hall in Nottingham of which we took the fullest advantage. With the war in Europe over at last, it was difficult to settle again to our normal activities.

The immediate future was now to pose some difficult problems. As might have been expected, the relations between the Western Powers and Soviet Russia were soon to turn sour. President Truman, successor to President Roosevelt, pushed aside the reconstruction loan which had been contemplated for the Soviet people. In the U.K., Parliament was in its tenth year. The Prime Minister had suggested that the coalition should continue until the war against Japan had been won, but Mr. Attlee offered to continue only for a maximum period of six months. Mr. Churchill declined to agree, at once resigning and bringing the National Government to an end. A General Election had been called for 5th July.

Early in June the Age and Service Release Group dates were

announced, arranged according to dates of birth and length of service. The older candidates were to be released first, and some of our colleagues qualified within a month. I had received private information from my immediate superior at A.A. Command that my name had gone forward two months previously for recommended promotion to Senior Commander. And now, suddenly, Colonel W., the officer in charge of Army Education sent instructions that I was to come to London for an interview.

"When are you due for release?" he asked.

"In November, Sir," I replied.

"Would you consider serving for a further six months, or a little longer? We desperately need experienced officers to help us carry out the great Army Educational Release scheme which is about to be launched."

With no other future in mind, and with the prospect of the erratic young woman L. about to return to Kirklands to help my father with his next book, I replied that I would be willing to consider a further six months of service in the A.T.S. The colonel appeared immensely relieved.

"You know your name is on the list for promotion. There will be a board shortly and then we will be able to let you know where we can best use you. I am very grateful."

We had all been granted a V.E. 48 hours leave, so I accepted Aunt Winnie's invitation to join her once again in Sheffield. She was greatly distressed that her daughter-in-law, Australian born and about to return to that country, had burnt all her son's clothes, books, letters, photographs and other possessions after his death in 1943. As next-of-kin this was her right, but Aunt Winnie regarded the act as utterly callous. Not unnaturally they had not got on. There was little I could say to comfort her.

It was now mid-summer with syringa blossoms making a milky way of stars and the newly lit street lamps shining like gold. Surrounding "Cloverlands" as the group headquarters was called, there was a charming garden with scent of lavender, mingled with mauve lilac and snow-white hawthorn. On my birthday evening I gave a little dinner party of special friends at the Nottingham Black Boy Hotel. The following morning I was touched to find my desk supporting two huge vases of summer flowers.

In York, the domestic science course for the A.T.S., which I had been organising for many weeks, became a reality. I stayed in the Y.W.C.A. Hostel, put at our disposal, watching the classes. The civilian instructors were admirable. Similar courses were to be run in Manchester and I was staying at Holly Royde when the General Election results, proving a veritable Labour party landslide, were announced.

There had been little or no interest in foreign affairs, certainly no agitation to extract reparations from Germany. It seemed as if the voters had cared only about their own future, housing, employment, and the new idea of life-long social security. The Labour party had offered a convincing manifesto. The Conservatives had been left far behind with the people cheering Churchill wherever he was seen but voting against him. It was thought that many votes had been lost by the former Prime Minister's speech, egged on by Lord Beaverbrook, that the future chairman of the Labour party might well become the sinister head of a British "Gestapo". "The Old Warrior is off course!" voters had said. Perhaps it was right for the country to have a complete change of government at that time. I remembered a Spanish saying of my dear mother, "No hay mal de que bien no venga." (There is no ill out of which some good does not come.)

On my return from Manchester, I received a much appreciated invitation from the general, through his A.D.C. daughter to come and dine with them at "Inglewood", their temporary home two miles from the group headquarters. "Father thought you might be depressed at the election result," she told me. "If you hurry you will be able to catch the duty car and W. (the general's driver) can drive you back to your billet."

We rarely talked politics, but this evening proved an exception. The general intensely disliked the Socialist theory about ending grammar schools and forcing the country to accept the new idea of comprehensive schooling. "It is supposed to bring about one nation, the widely held belief of Socialist supporters," I put in. "It is more likely to bring about ignorant, illiterate and quite possibly unemployable young people," the general retorted with surprising clairvoyance. Fortunately he was not to live long enough to rue the chaos now created in the heart of our great cities, mindless vandals, untaught, undisciplined, unskilled, without religion or morals. The bitter problem of immigration was, then, far away in the future.

Mr. Clement Attlee now took over as Prime Minister. In the wider world the Japanese campaign was being controlled largely by the American Chiefs of Staff. British and Commonwealth forces had been placed under American orders. American scientists had produced an atomic bomb ready for use, if need be, in the late summer of 1945. President Harry Truman had decided that the bombs should be used on two Japanese cities whose names are burnt into history, Hiroshima and Nagasaki. The Japanese surrendered. V.J. Day (15th August) brought the end of the war. Soon the overwhelming post-war troubles were to begin.

In September I received the summons to appear before the War Office Promotions Board. On the same day I had been electrified to get a letter from a dear neighbour and kind friend who lived in Headley, next door to Kirklands. The letter described a remarkable happening. It appeared that L., now re-established as my father's secretary, had been informing the villagers that she was soon expecting to marry my father. The Promotions Board allowed me to spend two nights in London so I booked a room at my club. My father's flat in St. James's Street had but one bedroom and he took all his meals in his own club, next door. He did, however, invite me to dinner where I placed the neighbour's letter before him.

"You mustn't take any notice," he reassured me. "L. is not quite stable and has fantasies. She is a brilliant stenographer and without her I couldn't finish my book. You see she is a girl with an absolutely negative personality. I couldn't dictate to a woman who glittered and glowed." I understood the position only too well.

"Well, I will keep away," I maintained, "I don't want to bring on one of her 'turns'." This upset my father who pressed me not to let her presence make any difference to my life. Obviously this was impossible, but as I still had a number of months to serve as an A.T.S. officer I felt the matter might well sort itself out.

My answers had evidently satisfied the board the following morning, and, in due course, I was given the information that I was to report to North West District, Preston, in the rank of Senior Commander (Major) at the beginning of October.

In my club that evening I was to meet my cousin, Patsy, who had started the herculean task of scrubbing out her Chelsea flat. With her was her nineteen-year-old sister, Gerry, radiantly happy over her recent engagement to a young R.A.F. officer.

CHAPTER TWENTY-TWO

After many goodbye parties at "Cloverlands", and after giving a thank-you present to the good hearted miner and his wife, whose spare room I had used, I loaded my car and drove to Preston. I was now on the last lap of my army career. In the darkening sky of an October evening no one could pretend that Preston was likely to present an exotic appearance, but, as I approached the smoking chimneys, the sun now quenched, and the outer countryside a hazy shadow, I felt I was entering a grimly ugly city. Even so, as my Sheffield grandfather had been known to exclaim, "You cannot forge the country's industry in a rose garden."

Soon I was to traverse the shiny greasy cobblestones of a road leading to the Drill Hall where the North West District headquarters had been established. It was to turn out that the Education Office, always the "Cinderella" of army life, had been pushed into a squalid corner of the town and I was quite unprepared for what I was now to find. The house was filthy. It had peeling wall-paper and rickety stairs. Books, files and papers, littered the floor and dirty coffee cups had been stranded along dusty mantelpieces. In the hall someone had placed a bucket to catch the rain dripping through a leaking ceiling. I felt quite appalled. How on earth can they work in such surroundings, I wondered. I was taken to meet the Lancastrian Colonel H., my new colleague, a man of warmth and kindness, and his assistant, Captain B., also an officer who was to become a sterling friend.

"Don't worry about the appearance of this dreadful house," said Colonel H., sensing my disgust, "We are soon to move. We shall be absorbed in huts now being built behind the Drill Hall." That, at least, sounded a consolation.

The requisitioned house in West Cliff, serving as the joint officers' mess, was very dismal, but at least it had a garage enabling me to put my car under cover. We numbered sixteen of whom seven were A.T.S., a remarkable change from the enormous crowd I had become accustomed to in Chester and Kimberley. My fellow officers addressed me as "Ma'am" which was quite a shock. The seniority, however, did give me the advantage of a single room.

On my first morning I received a most generous letter of thanks and appreciation from my former General B. Happily I was to keep in touch with him for many years in the civilian world. I greatly missed the bonhomie and togetherness of the A.A. Groups.

By daylight, the Army Educational headquarters looked even more sordid. In the dim light of the previous evening I had not observed the rotting floorboards and cobwebs grey with years hanging from old disused gas brackets. Some of the shelves were inches thick with dust and mildew.

"How long have you been here?" I asked Subaltern W., the rather surly A.T.S. officer who was to be my assistant.

"Several months," came the reply.

"I wonder you haven't made an effort to clean this place up," I commented, thus earning her disapproval. Fortunately, with the help of the staff we all got this terrible house spring-cleaned in the course of the first week, a relief to us all.

Now I had a bigger problem on hand. How to keep the mass of A.T.S. happy, keen and interested until their respective demobilisation dates were arrived at. I began to study the lay-out of this completely new area. Having been stationed in Chester I was at least familiar with the local roads.

In the snow-bound winter of 1942, as a sergeant in Camberley, I had given a number of talks embodying the country's past. I remembered that these had been enjoyed. Throughout the war, Mr. Churchill had always referred to "Our Island Race". If I could now find enough instructors to conduct courses of the occasions in history when the people had not despaired, these might prove fresh. Earlier leaders than Churchill had given the British nation faith to endure. I put the suggestion to Colonel H.

"You go ahead, m'dear, the A.T.S. is your responsibility. Whatever you decide you will have my blessing."

Fortunately I already knew many of the regional officers from Manchester and Liverpool. These good people collaborated with enthusiasm, especially as I had undertaken to give many of the talks myself. Quite soon I had laid the foundation for a whole series of courses, the new Norman Order, the creation of Grand Juries, the Justices of the Peace, the Knights of the Shire, the Tradesmen of the Boroughs, the Church, and the Crown. It was to be the whole pattern of society leading to Parliament and the final alliance between Crown and Commons. Captain B., my new assistant, expressed keen interest. "If the courses go well, do you think some of the men could take part?" "I can't see why they shouldn't," I answered, "Provided enough space can be made available." Very soon my project was under way.

The weeks passed. Returning from Carlisle through the Lake District I noticed that winter was at hand. The bare trees seemed to be alive with restless breezes and, out of the wind, the gleaming lakes shone like silver spoons. I was thankful for my car and for my position as an authorised petrol user. As a pre-war Londoner, I had seen little of the glorious English and Scottish countryside this war job had provided. For me personally, this had been Hilter's bonus!

With the coming of Christmas, my father had despatched L. to stay with a sister in Yorkshire. He had been particularly anxious that I should join him for my few days leave. Although almost three years had passed since my mother's death, Kirklands seemed desolate without her. On this occasion Aunt Floss had gone to visit her daughter so my father suggested that we should travel together to London to see a pantomime. London looked battered and dreary although work was now in hand to blot out the appalling blemish of bomb damage.

I spent a weekend with my hospitable brother and family before returning to Preston. The children looked fit and sturdy, a great tribute, not only to their mother's devoted care, but to Lord Woolton's rationing. Despite the end of the war, rationing remained, indeed some food, together with clothing and other items had become even scarcer and taxation was soon to rise sharply.

Mr. Attlee's Goverment were rushing ahead with their promised legislative programme in the spheres of nationalisation and social services. There was an acute shortage of housing, and the cost of securing free medical care for all citizens was soon to put a heavier strain on the Exchequer than the Labour Government had anticipated.

The new year of 1946 now opened with bitterly cold winds and the ground iron-hard. Our Education office, together with the officers' mess now moved into a series of huts with pleasant wide windows. We were all delighted. The work of "homemaking" and "handicraft" continued, and my history courses were proving popular. The colonel and I went on tour together. Despite his "rough diamond" appearance, he was a very kind man and I grew to appreciate his sound common sense and pleasant company. He, like Major H., proved a most companionable fellow-worker. He always backed me with the utmost loyalty.

In March, my particularly difficult and unco-operative fellow officer, Subaltern W., was posted. Her replacement, Subaltern Joan C., her opposite in every way, worked with great diligence and I never had a more loyal, convivial or trustworthy companion. Joan was to devote her future to the A.T.S. or W.R.A.C. as it was soon to be called, and I am glad to feel that we are still in touch.

Army affairs were rapidly winding down. A new development had emerged, the formation of what were to become called "Extra Colleges". These Formation Colleges offered a month's course to all ranks with the choice of three subjects. Set up in various centres, it was thought that those in the north and particularly in Scotland offered the most satisfactory surroundings. Accordingly, I put my name forward for New Battle Abbey, Dalkeith, with the hope of studying political philosophy, history and sewing. In a few days, information reached me that my name had been accepted for a course in July.

And now for the first time since 1935 my father's Imperial Press conference, under its revised name of Commonwealth Press Union, was to meet in London. As formerly, delegates were to be entertained as lavishly as the stringent conditions allowed, with visits to the Provinces. The Lord Mayor of Liverpool had undertaken to act as host in the Civic Hall. Delegates were to stay in the Adelphi Hotel. My father had sent a ticket enabling me to join him in what proved to be a particularly memorable occasion. His recently published book *Pilgrims and Pioneers* had been widely praised and he himself was called upon to make an admirable speech. He had been the founder and inaugurator of the original conference in the summer of 1909. The local press gave the conference generous support. There were many kind newspaper articles praising my father's far-seeing conception.

I was only to be called upon to give three more talks to the now rapidly disbanding A.T.S. units on the War Office subject "Rebuilding for Peace". And so, after my thank-you party for the many who had helped me in North West District, I embarked on the train to Scotland, leaving my car in a local garage. I still had to return for my "medical" and to collect my A.T.S. release book with its many documents.

In Dalkeith, New Battle Abbey proved to be an imposing building said to have been erected by monks in the fifthteenth century and now updated. There was little left of the once tenderly nurtured garden sadly spoilt by the sprawling cohorts of army huts. I was joined in a two-room bedroom by a fellow senior commander who was taking the courses of institutional management, book-keeping and painting. Separated during the day, we were able to enjoy one another's company after work often visiting Edinburgh where we enjoyed exploring that lovely city.

I was the only pupil for my subject of political philosophy experiencing what would now be called a one to one tutorial, with an engaging professor from Glasgow University. I found it exceptionally interesting and made great progress. History was a bigger class and here I met a pleasant young man called John Cartland, who became a friend. I was to meet him again in the civilian world. In the sewing class, I managed to produce a reasonably attractive blouse. It had always been a great regret that I had not inherited my mother's gift with her needle.

The whole course proved very worthwhile with cheerful entertainment in the evenings, drama groups, music, reel clubs, dances, films; and at the weekends there were rambles, tennis and golf, for those whose enjoyment turned to exercise. At the end of July I now journeyed back to Preston for my final release, seriously wondering what the future held in store.

CHAPTER TWENTY-THREE

Demobilised at last, I looked out of Kirklands window. August 1946 had reached the rich splendour of high summer with its brilliant light and gracious shadows. In the Hampshire countryside the corn was high in the fields. Aeons of time seemed to have passed since my first night at Camberley. L. was out of the way, but only temporarily. I knew my father longed to get on with his book. If only I could find somewhere to live in London, I thought. And then, almost as if taking me by the hand, luck stepped in again, and I received a telephone call. It proved to be one of my oldest friends, Joan W., then staying in a Frensham cottage with her two young sons. Joan worked in M.I.5 and lived in a block of flats called Kensington Close (now a hotel). It transpired that a flat might become vacant and Joan advised me to contact the secretary in charge of lettings to tenants. I acted swiftly, rejoicing in the reply that a flat might possibly become available some time in September.

With my father accompanying me I went to see the flats where the amenities were admirable; restaurant, swimming bath, squash courts, various bars and snack bars, and basement garage. The flats themselves were provided with radio and telephone, private bathroom but no actual kitchen. I could hardly believe my sudden good fortune.

Meanwhile, with a little petrol saved, I accepted a kind invitation from my cousin, Julia, to meet my attractive three-months-old god-daughter, Angela, in their Exmouth home. Angela was very engaging, regarding me with round surprised eyes as she lay and watched me from her "Moses" basket. After so long in uniform, it was pleasant to be back again in the normal world.

The gentle countryside of South Devon, with its balmy air, soft light and cosy red earth looked uniquely lovely as Julia and I drove towards Dundridge. Invited to lunch by my aunt and uncle we had taken three-year-old Patrick whose copper head bobbed about among the hydrangeas. The family were struggling hard with almost no staff to keep the well-loved house and garden in order. The change in Dundridge underlined how entirely obsolete the pre-war world of my youth had now become. As the French were to put it succinctly "Les Milords c'est fini!"

Nevertheless we *had* won the war and Aunt Sybil proudly showed us photographs of the new grandchildren. My W.R.N.S. cousins Pamela and Olivia, both married in the preceding year, had produced one daughter apiece. The sons were to come later. Uncle Emile and Aunt Sybil were still indefatigable with their public work although the former had now retired from politics.

Before returning to Kirklands, I paid a visit to Great Aunt Lottie, my grandfather's last remaining sister, who was very much of a family favourite. In her late eighties she had settled into the Riverside Hotel at Bovey Tracey. To her immense grief she had recently received news of the death of one of her granddaughters, Daphne, from meningitis. Daphne, a charming girl, married and with a baby son, had had everything to live for. It seemed a tragic waste. There was happy news, however, about Joan and Audrey the older granddaughters. Audrey, married and abroad, was later to present Aunt Lottie with two great granddaughters. The Harvey family tree seemed to be widening.

Aunt Floss, in her hotel in Froyle, invited me over for the day soon after my return expressing her concern about L. "A most unstable young woman I understand." I replied that I warmly agreed, ardently wishing that my father would find a replacement.

With the first sign of autumn-bronzed leaves, thanks to my kind friend, Joan, now back at her job in M.I.5, I was allotted a flat in Kensington Close. Despite its diminutive size, and utility furniture, I felt overwhelmingly proud and pleased. At last I had a place of my own! With L's imminent return to Kirklands this seemed imperative. Both my father and my brother came to dine with me in the attractive restaurant. I even took up swimming again. It was my first total independence.

Post-war London was a tragic sight and it was to be years before the bomb damage was finally concealed. We were all shabbily dressed and the food was dreary. The Labour Government were still obliged to take very harsh measures.

Walking along Kensington High Street one October morning I ran into an old friend and colleague of pre-war years, Rosemary W-E. "Well, how splendid to see you!" she exclaimed. "Are you living in London again or just visiting?"

"By wonderful luck," I answered, "I've just settled into Kensington Close where I have a small flat. A good friend pulled strings. I have only been demobilised since August."

"Well you're just the sort of candidate for the Kensington Borough Council," she told me. She herself was chairman of various committees and had served for some years.

"There is a vacancy for the Brompton Ward with a by-election coming up. How would it appeal to you? Come and have tea with me in Iverna Gardens and I can tell you about it." The meeting resulted in my being passed by a committee and I became a candidate. To my surprise I had neither rival nor opponent and was shortly to find myself a borough councillor, having been returned unopposed. With my interest in politics this seemed a happy chance and was to prove a valuable bottom rung. In addition, I was to make many new friends.

The work of the borough council was not onerous and I had time on my hands. I had been lucky enough to have inherited a small family legacy so the need for rushing into full-time employment had not been urgent, but, as winter drew on, I felt I must start searching for a permanent job. There were, of course, thousands of former service members all seeking employment, many in the London area. Having applied to various agencies, leaving my name, I enrolled for a six-weeks' course of cooking at the Good Housekeeping Institute. In all the many domestic science courses I had organised for the A.T.S. I had not had time to participate.

This was an enjoyable course, but the rations were so limited, dried eggs, powdered milk, very little fat, no sugar, and almost invisible meat, that the class faced a certain thinness of recipes. The generosity of army rations had made the A.T.S. courses more valuable.

In this dying year of 1946 the theatres remained vigorously alive. For a short time both plays and actors seemed to achieve an unusually high standard, until the demand for a totally fresh style of drama was to come about. Preferring to avoid visiting Kirklands, I made great use of the 2.30 Saturday afternoon matinées often inviting friends. Mr. Attlee and his team were making their "great leap forward" along the path of social reform. The opposition, now the Conservative party, after the shock of losing the 1945 election so disastrously, were reorganising their whole machinery. There was, however, much trouble on the economic front and the new Britain desperately hoping to thrust its way through the war ruins was to be held up by the shortage and expensiveness of raw material. Even harsher measures of domestic restriction were soon to be undertaken by the austere Chancellor of the Exchequer, Sir Stafford Cripps. The generous Americans were providing enormous help for Europe under the "Marshall Plan".

At the beginning of December, distressed by my avoidance of Kirklands, my father telephoned.

"*Do* come for the next weekend," he enjoined. I agreed, on the understanding that if anything went wrong with L. I would leave immediately.

"I don't want to cause trouble," I stressed, "As I know you find her useful but she is obviously deeply hostile to me. I only have to appear for her 'fur' to rise!"

"She can't help it, poor thing, it is a mental affliction, and she is the best stenographer I have found. I really do need her until I have got this book into print."

As promised, I arrived at Kirklands for the weekend. L. flashed me a look of fiendish hatred. I had barely removed my coat before all the pent up jealousy came flooding out. It seemed that she deeply resented my army career, felt enormously aggravated because I had acquired a London flat in a matter of weeks; "And now even the Kensington Borough Council has fallen into your lap, you didn't even have to contest the seat." On and on she shrieked in the same vein. I refrained from replying. My silence maddened her further, and she then screamed at my father, "You kicked me, you kicked me!" He watched horrified, still glued to his chair. The arrival of a tea tray broke the spell and she rushed to her room, a hideous scowl of fury on her face. Fortunately for the whole household she took to her bed.

"How can you stand it?" I queried. "She is obviously very sick and needs medical help." My father nodded.

"I think she is dangerous, she might set fire to the house," I continued. "She only has these 'turns' very occasionally," he answered, but he was quite shaken. In London again I telephoned the local doctor. "I know about it," he said, "And it worries me but your father wants her there."

"She is certainly not a 'femme fatale'," I remarked to my kind friend, Joan, describing the whole unpleasant incident a few days later as we shared our nightcap of Ovaltine in Joan's cosy flat. Ovaltine had remained unrationed. "But it does mean that I will have to stay away from Kirklands until my father's book is finished and I do resent this. If only he would find another secretary."

"Wouldn't your dear mother be grieved?" came the sympathetic response. "It seems the kind of situation for a bad novel!" I wound up.

In the London parks the last leaves had fallen and the bonfires were burning low. The fading bronze and purple chrysanthemums suggested that the grey weeks of winter were drawing closer. Even so, London at night, after groping about in the dark for so many years, seemed like a glittering fairyland. One or two remaining bachelor friends of my younger years invited me to a dance or perhaps visit a theatre. Kensington Close undertook a monthly dinner-dance in its attractive restaurant and even the Ladies' Carlton rose to the occasion putting on a Christmastime Ball. My brother and wife, together with a few old friends, joined my party. Peggy, my sister-in-law, looked very frail. Certainly the young "mums" with small children had had a much harder war than those of us who had joined the women's services.

I was now a member of the Kensington Borough Council Libraries' Committee which I was enjoying but the council work was not without some expense and in those days there were no allowances. A little extra dropped into my budget, I thought, would prove very agreeable. Once more I pressed the secretary of the London Appointments Board to be sure to let me know if any suitable job should appear on her books.

CHAPTER TWENTY-FOUR

The New Year of 1947 was to bring the severest winter for over sixty years. Icy winds blew, temperatures dropped below zero, blizzards raged, coal stocks disappeared, gas pressure was sharply reduced, electricity was minimal, and soon heat and light were to vanish altogether for set periods in the day. A snowy blanket several feet deep appeared to cover the whole country. Industry became paralysed, snowdrifts created immense transport hold-ups, and the appalling losses in livestock were soon to produce an unparalleled crisis in agriculture. Tragically many birds were caught up in this desperate winter, dying of starvation and thirst.

At the height of this most calamitous February, my brother's wife was swept into hospital for a serious operation. Immediately he begged me to come and help. On the same day the London Appointments Board advised me to apply for a job on the staff of an organisation newly established called "Federated States of Europe". Obviously I had to decline the job. Peggy had always shown me the utmost kindness over so many years, even bringing a beautiful bunch of flowers, complete with its own vase, to present to me on my first morning in Kensington Close. My brother, too, had done so much for me in my life. Their children needed care. I pulled my dyed army greatcoat, the only winter coat I possessed, out of the cupboard, packed a bag, and set off to Rickmansworth.

There were no clothing coupons available for wellington boots, (even if there had been any in the shops) but an extremely kind neighbour lent me a pair of snowshoes. She had even prepared the children's supper for which I was inordinately grateful. The next weeks became a nightmare. Had I been the type to get braced up with alcoholic drinks to deaden the nerves, this would have been the right occasion!

After nearly a month of queueing in the biting wind to collect the pitifully meagre family rations, which all had to be cooked in advance because of the power cuts; and the effort of getting the children to school warmly fed and clothed, I heard with the utmost thankfulness that another exceptionally good-hearted neighbour had offered to take them both under her wing until arrangements could be made to send them to a temporary boarding school. The hospital news was good enabling me to take the children to visit their mother, who was now out of danger. The relief was immense as my responsibility ended.

In London again, the bitter cold continued with the staff of shops and offices struggling to carry out their work by candlelight. Towards the end of March I received a further letter from the London Appointments Board, asking me if I would be interested in applying for the post of secretary to the general secretary and medical director of the "National Association for Mental Health". Joining a large number of applicants at the address given, 39 Queen Anne Street, fate and luck joined hands with me again and I was appointed, meeting the very delightful general secretary, a Mr. Ormond, and his medical secretary colleague, a well-known psychiatrist. Back in my flat, I read the reports that the nightmare winter had turned to spring with such appalling floods that some villagers were watching thick lumps of ice sweeping along their streets. Many rivers now burst their banks causing several roads to become impassable.

My brother, now at the Joint Services Staff College, had bought a farm in Cornwall, where he was able to take his wife for the latter part of her convalescence. After a seemingly preposterous delay the radiant green of a very late spring and the prospect of summer foliage burst through at last, to cheer the country folk still grappling with the recent winter disaster.

The new job I had undertaken would have been more accurately described as "office management". The house in Queen Anne Street urgently in need of redecorating proved dark and dismal. The hall, piled up with immense boxes of discarded books and files, led to five further floors. There was no lift and I was horrified to discover the number of staff crushed together in some rooms. Wherever I looked, letters, papers, documents and files, appeared to be cluttered around in wild confusion. "The National Association for Mental Health" it was explained to me, had recently absorbed two similar organisations running separately, and none wanted to make their individual staff redundant, hence the overcrowding. In addition, there seemed to be considerable jealousy, suspicion and ill-feeling, between the various sections.

In the basement I discovered old filing cabinets, trunks, bicycles, and rusting filing trays half buried in a shambles of books. It was disconcerting. My internal telephone rang incessantly with querulous requests for further stationery, additional electric light bulbs, or petulantly calling my attention to a leak in a gas pipe, a broken window or a dripping tank. It was also my task to supervise the general secretary's mail and to enter the medical director's appointments in his diary.

I had two assistants, one a very flighty little person who cared nothing whatever for the job, and the second an admirable young woman who had been a W.R.E.N. Shortly after my arrival preparations began to take place for the annual general meeting with my assistants feverishly "rolling off" interminable notes on a machine called "Banda" even more antiquated than the monster I

The end of one of Goering's Luftwaffe. Plate 14

had been called upon to use in my days as a "clerk" at Crawley Rise. Then, as if to make amends for the cruel winter, an almost perpetual summer heatwave got under way.

The summer of 1947 was to prove one of the hottest on record. By July I had managed to get some order out of the chaotic conditions in 39 Queen Anne Street even persuading some of the staff to give me a hand with washing, dusting and polishing which seemed reminiscent of my efforts in the Education Headquarters at Preston. Unfiled letters were at last in order, documents labelled and the litter removed. Many of the staff showed their appreciation, but the quarrels and disagreements between the sections continued and I found myself acting as a sort of clearing centre. Mr. Ormond was remarkably kind but the medical director gave me some worry as his letters were so frequently pushed aside and left unanswered. As a psychiatrist he worked for long hours outside the association headquarters which he obviously preferred. In due course I took to answering his letters myself. With a smile he said, "Thank-you very much," and signed without comment. It was a relief.

With the last of my petrol coupons I made my way to visit the two children in their school near Buckingham, taking their delayed birthday presents. We now had the splendid news that their mother's health was really improving and I was able to buoy them up with hope that their return home was likely to be soon. They looked well, but worried, and had grown out of their clothes, but at least they had been provided with food and shelter, some kind of education and the companionship of other children who appeared to be overwhelmingly small boys. This situation did not seem to perturb my friendly young niece.

My brother had now taken a house at Chesham Bois, having decided to leave Rickmansworth. The children were on the point of being entered for permanent boarding schools having then reached the ages of ten and eight, one to Quarr House, Sway, and the other to Hawtrey's. My poor young nephew was never to enjoy his prep. school life.

CHAPTER TWENTY-FIVE

In the outside world the communist parties, with Russian support, had seized power in Hungary, Bulgaria, Rumania and Poland. Now a Cominform was created, an organisation whose avowed object was to fight and destroy the political systems of the West. At the end of the war it had been hopefully expected that the three major powers, Britain, America and Russia would have been able to co-operate together in the shaping of the post-war world, but this was not to be.

Towards the end of July, by the kindness of the Lord Chamberlain, my name had been included on my father's invitation to the Royal Garden Party. Mr. Ormond gave me the day off. I had had some trouble in finding a dress suitable to wear, as strict clothes rationing continued, but a friend had recommended a newly established dressmaker in Church Street, who was good enough to remake a pre-war dress which I had had dyed. Synthetic materials were still in the future. Unrationed hats, however, were fully available.

Accompanying my father I enjoyed the first Royal Garden Party I was in a position to attend since 1939. There was much excitement over the recently announced engagement of H.R.H. Princess Elizabeth to Lieutenant Philip Mountbatten, R.N. Mr. Churchill was not present, to the disappointment of a French visitor who told my father, "You have no idea of the significance of that great man's voice in the bleak misery and wretchedness of occupied France. He was our one shining beacon of hope." Old friends such as Mr. Leo Amery joined us in the tea tent where there was an overpowering smell of mothballs. Much interest was being centred on the new possibility of European Unity in which Mr. Churchill was taking a leading part.

It was generally supposed that the majority of the Labour Cabinet were in favour of a United Europe, but one or two had expressed doubt. The story was related of Mr. Ernie Bevin's delightful remark, "Once you open that Pandora's box you don't know what kind of Trojan 'orses are likely to jump out." Mr. Churchill had invented the phrase, "The Iron Curtain", and another unusual situation, "The Cold War", was shortly to become evident. Many politicians worried about the agreement at the Potsdam Conference, with Germany, shorn of East Prussia, divided into four zones of occupation, U.S.A., British, French and Russian, with Berlin deep in the Russian zone. It was becoming clearer that all areas in the Russian zone were to become part of a Red Empire. In due course the former allies were to merge their zones in the west to create the West German Federal Republic. A year later negotiations were to begin for a North Atlantic Treaty Organisation despite the traditional American policy of no political entanglement with Europe.

In this August of 1947 the thermometer touched the nineties. Mr. Ormond decreed that the staff should have a mid-morning break for iced-drinks so we all went out together into Wigmore Street sitting at pavement tables under coloured sunshades at a little place appropriately called "The Orange Tree". The rush hour had become more and more unpleasant and now with the Proms restarted in the Albert Hall after their war break, it was easier to wait until late. Some of us joined together for an evening meal at a pleasant restaurant in Welbeck Street which had the delightful name of "The Ambrosia". The swimming bath at Kensington Close was a great boon and a happy way of entertaining some kind friends. The affairs of the Kensington Borough Council had now gone into abeyance until October.

As this very hot summer gave way to autumn, I was due for a brief holiday. Distressed at my continual refusal to come to Kirklands as long as L. was in the cottage, my father made the suggestion that he and I should go on a brief holiday on our own. Basic petrol was now minimal and was about to be withdrawn altogether, "but I think I have enough for a brief car tour," my father declared. So we made our plans.

Stopping in Gloucester in the beautiful fourteenth century coaching inn, called, perhaps a little unsuitably, "The New Inn", my father invited his old friend the dean, a former headmaster of Westminster School, to join us for dinner. Accompanied by his delightful wife they reminded me of the time when, at the age of eleven, I had burst into the headmaster's den to seek permission to use the old wall for practising lacrosse during the boys' school holidays. "We did admire you!" his wife told me. "You were *so* small but with such self-confidence and such shining bright eyes!" "I was amazed at your energy," put in her distinguished husband. "People used to ask 'who was the little girl with the long plaits so fleet-footed chasing her ball?'" "It was extremely kind of you to give me permission," I answered, "And your kindness paid off handsomely enabling me to win my team lacrosse colours in long-ago school days."

The dean was in high spirits relating two favourite stories. One was of a small girl who had inquired of her mother after her father had left for work, "Mummy, if daddy died, would he go to heaven?" The reply came at once, "Oh! darling, how could you ever imagine such a crazy idea!" The second related to a little boy questioning his grandfather. "Grandpapa, were you in the Ark?" "Well no, old chap, I wasn't actually in the Ark." "Then how did you manage not to get drowned?"

My father's additional story was not without charm. "A six-year-old had been taken by her aunt and uncle on a visit to the zoo. Entranced with the chimpanzees the child had exclaimed, "Oh! isn't that one exactly like Uncle Bertram?" "Hush, dear," came the horrified reply. "You mustn't say that, you'll hurt his feelings." "But Auntie," persisted the child, "Surely monkeys can't understand?"

The dean was very entertaining and we spent a cheerful and most enjoyable evening, accompanying him the following morning on a tour of the glorious Gloucester Cathedral. In the autumn sunshine the old yew trees hung their heavy evergreen boughs over ancient tombstones.

Our drive through the lovely countryside of Herefordshire and then into Wales took us at length to Tenby where we had booked rooms for the night in the Tenby Hotel. Arriving as the sun was setting like an old-fashioned chinese lantern, we watched seagulls swooping and chattering over an olive-dark sea. At length rose-tinged clouds, blushing with the afterglow, brought ribbons of milky mist soon to turn the purple horizon into a grey smudge.

A day later, my father's friend, Major Gwilym Lloyd George, son of the famous statesman, one of the few Liberals still in

Parliament, gave us an entertaining commentary on the up-to-date political scene over a hospitable lunch to which he and his cordial wife had invited us. He related one unflattering little story about the then Prime Minister. "Mr. Attlee took a taxi to 10 Downing Street. The taxi door swung open but no one got out!"

We moved north to Aberystwyth circling back to Llandrindod Wells through the unique landscape glowing with the ever-changing variety of mountains, lakes and rivers. Across the border in England we stopped in an enchanting inn near Worcester with welcoming beamed ceiling, glistening polished brass and log fire.

Homeward bound, the next morning, we stopped at Oxford for lunch. With rationed petrol there was little traffic and the "City of Dreaming Spires" appeared soaked in peace. The weather, however, had changed and in the peaceful seclusion of Worcester College gardens, the rain ran like quicksilver down the shining leaves of the old holly tree.

Lunching in the Randolph Hotel, I was surprised to meet my former colleague from New Battle Abbey, John Cartland, just taking up a post with the Oxford Appointments Board. Joining us for coffee, he embarked on an immediate conversation while my father, having waited for the rain to clear, disappeared into his beloved college gardens.

"I'm so glad to meet you again. I wanted to write but had no idea of your address. After you had left Dalkeith, your Glasgow professor impressed upon me that you were a 'natural' as a parliamentary candidate." With a smile I let him continue. "There is a vacancy for a Conservative candidate at Willesden, would you feel like considering it?" Here I had to answer. "I think it would be financially impossible just at the moment." In fact, careful reinvesting of my family legacy had recently made me economically independent, but with too small a margin for the huge expense of standing for Parliament.

"It is extremely good of you to think of me," I told him, "And I do hope we may keep in touch." On my father's return we proceeded on the last stage of our journey.

With the wind now squally and energetic, and in the silver greyness of rain, we drove south on our return to London.

"Where did you meet that pleasant young man?" my father inquired. "He was in charge of one of the history syndicates when I was at Dalkeith in July 1946," I responded. I then added, "He is a Worcester College graduate, I understand he pulled off a 'First'. He was inviting me to become a parliamentary candidate saying that there was a vacancy in Willesden."

"What did you tell him?" "I replied that I could not really afford it." My father's next reaction voiced my own feelings.

"To be an M.P. you need all possible co-operation from a wife, together with a full-time secretary and a stack of money. Even if Willesden were to prove winnable, and that is most uncertain, it would be a tremendously hard struggle for a woman alone."

The car sped on. On the outskirts of Beaconsfield, a gleam of sun having pierced the clouds, we stopped for tea. In a charming garden we admired age-twisted fruit trees, with autumn-bronzed leaves, purple michaelmas daisies, flame coloured nasturtiums and honey-scented buddleia over which the last of the summer butterflies hovered with rainbow wings.

In a pearl-grey haze, with rain in a thin damp drizzle like a mesh of fine silk, we moved on towards the end of our holiday. It had made a most delightful country change from my London surroundings. I wished fervently that my father might get his book completed, or better still, procure another secretary. Happily this situation was not to prove so far ahead as I had supposed.

CHAPTER TWENTY-SIX

Clearing my last letter in my office at 39 Queen Anne Street one October evening, I was surprised by a knock at the door. It proved to be the congress manager for the International Congress on Mental Health, due to take place in London in the spring of 1948. I had met the manager at committee meetings.

"I came to ask if you would like to join my staff for the coming congress as press-publicity officer?" he stated.

"I think it would be an honour," I replied. "But I will need to discuss it, both with Mr. Ormond, and with the medical director."

"Well, of course," he said, "But let me know soon. We have acquired an office at 19 Manchester Street."

I had grown very fond of Mr. Ormond and also of the medical director in my months as their joint secretary. Both advised me to take the offer. "It may well lead on to something better." Both expressed their appreciation for the miracle they agreed I had brought about by sorting out the chaos in the whole building. I assured them that I had enjoyed the job and had indeed felt grateful for the chance of undertaking it.

Accordingly, arrangements were put in hand for my replacement. The congress manager invited me to lunch and we agreed that I should join his staff at 19 Manchester Street at the end of November.

I had not expected that any of the staff would mind my leaving so I was really touched to find an enormous bouquet of flowers on my desk on my last morning with the message inserted, "Best of luck. Please keep in touch, we shall all miss you very much." I was gratified at the very kind thought. There was to be a gap of a few days between the end of one job and the beginning of the next which enabled me to join the happy crowd jostling around Buckingham Palace on the eve of Princess Elizabeth's wedding. The country was still under rationing and severe restrictions but the

Palace had been bathed in a glow of light and there were a few fireworks. The following morning, standing in the Mall under fluttering flags, I watched the young Princess at her father's side, a shimmering vision, waving from the famous glass coach. A great crescendo of cheering and magnificent pealing of bells accompanied her to the irreplaceable Westminster Abbey which seems to have borne the weight of history through all our centuries.

"What did she look like?" asked one of my colleagues later.

"Like a fairy tale," I answered. "Magnetic and dazzling, all white and silver, gleaming and sparkling with a mass of what looked like lacy frothy tulle." This happy event lifted us all temporarily from the post-war dreariness.

The following week I reported to 19 Manchester Street to start one of the most unrewarding jobs I have ever tackled. Making a great effort to contact all publicity centres, I met with little success. In the sombre aftermath of war the press were searching for uplifting tidings. Money was scarce and the economy still dire. The subject of mental health was depressing, particularly in poor bomb-shattered cities, some complete wastelands, where there was, as yet, no money to hide the scars. Our office, too, presented every sort of discomfort, the hired furniture proved useless, lights went out, radiators refused to grow warm and the plumbing was deplorable.

After a short time, the congress manager asked me to come and see him.

"I know this is not what you had in mind," he said apologetically. "But will you take on the 'office management' as well as publicity? I need someone experienced and the job will entail procuring and interviewing staff. There is an immense amount of work to be undertaken if we are to succeed." Very reluctantly I agreed.

The staff problem proved anything but easy. New typists were barely literate and while one tried to make allowances for the evacuated school children the majority were unemployable. One stroke of luck came my way in the most unlikely person of an office cleaner. This candidate had been a librarian but eye trouble had obliged her to shoulder remarkably different work. She became a tower of strength helping me with all the abominable troubles of sorting out difficulties which seemed unending.

It was my task to visit the Central Hall, Westminster, staking a claim for the days chosen in which this particular congress was due to take place in the spring of 1948. The building itself was full of "ghosts" for me personally. It was here that my mother's National Festival of Song had taken place year after year in the 1920s and 1930s. In my mind's eye I could see the enthusiastic competitors for solo and group singing, the really splendid amateur choirs, the fine piano players, and the excellent recitation performers. I could picture the generous adjudicators giving their time freely, together with all the efficient administrative staff. And, by no means least, the popular Mrs. Stanley Baldwin, as she then was, handing out the magnificent winning cups, shields and prizes, greatly encouraging the members of the pre-war Conservative Associations, who had worked so hard. My mother's gentle and much-loved personality still seemed to linger in the empty rooms.

Aunt Winnie arrived in London for Christmas stopping at the Kensington De Vere Hotel. Happy to be able to repay a little of her abundant hospitality to me in my A.T.S. years, I prevailed upon her to be my guest on several occasions and together we visited some enthralling plays.

Early in the New Year, Earl Baldwin died. As an old family friend, my father asked me to accompany him to the memorial service in Westminster Abbey. Quite by chance I found myself sitting next to a life-long political colleague of my father, Sir Herbert Williams, at that time the Member of Parliament for Croydon. I had known Sir Herbert since my very young days. In Dean's Yard after the service he took my arm. "I have often thought of you," he told me, "And I would like you to come and lunch with me tomorrow at the Conservative Club." Explaining that I was then on the staff of the International Congress and had already taken time off for Lord Baldwin's service, he at once suggested, "Well, come for dinner instead. I've known you since you were in white socks so you can look on me as an uncle!"

At dinner the following night in Sir Herbert's club, he came straight to the point. "I know you are already a member of the Kensington Borough Council," he said, "But I think you should go much further. How would you feel about standing for the London County Council, you are just the right candidate?"

"It would appeal to me very much," I responded, "Particularly as my present job is purely temporary and far from enjoyable."

"Good," he retorted. "Then may I send your name forward?" I expressed my thanks. He continued, "Good women candidates are rare and women councillors are eagerly sought, but you needn't bother for the moment, the next election is in April 1949." I certainly felt very appreciative of his kind suggestion.

As the year of 1948 moved on, my job at 19 Manchester Street became more and more disagreeable. The congress manager was beginning to get flustered, duplicating orders to different members of the staff and causing great confusion. The poor typists were now inundated with countless hundreds of envelopes which required addressing but with no list of procurable addresses. Even the envelopes already addressed became muddled. To add to our discomfort the radiators were now so hot that we could hardly endure them and the windows had stuck fast becoming completely immoveable. We shared our thankfulness that the congress would be over in the spring.

Meanwhile, I received a letter from the secretary of the London Municipal Society (now discontinued) that my name had been included in the list of potential L.C.C. candidates for the forthcoming election of April 1949. Very shortly afterwards another letter reached me from the general secretary of Ashridge, the former Bonar Law Memorial College. The letter read, "We hear from Mr. John Cartland that you were engaged as a lecturer for some part of your time in the A.T.S. women's service. We are running a course over Easter on the subject of 'The Great Ages of England' and wonder if we can interest you in taking on one of the syndicates?" This sounded most pleasant and I determined that, as my job in helping forward this congress was so nearly completed, I would ask to leave at the end of March. A most surprising letter from the office cleaner reached me after my departure which gave me great pleasure. "I was deeply sad to hear that you were leaving us. In this heartless age it is wonderful to find someone as consistently kind, courteous and considerate as you have been. You showed such tact and charm and you really brightened up my life. I do wish you good luck in all your future."

It was to be a radiantly lovely Easter at Ashridge, the delightful Elizabethan manor house close to Berkhamsted. Some of my talks given to the A.T.S. entitled "Our Island Race" were fully useable to my pleasant, lively syndicate. In the afternoons we took our exercise in the beautiful woodlands watching the clouds change pattern against the sun, admiring the pigeon-egg blue of a spring skyline and listening to the enchanting birdsong. The evenings brought keen discussions about world affairs.

After three years the popularity of Socialist planning was declining. Shortages had produced a "black market" with spivs, as they were called, gathering to sell rationed commodities. Disillusion was beginning to creep in.

The day after my return a letter summoned me to appear before a board at the headquarters of the London Municipal Society with a view to being selected as a potential L.C.C. candidate. The board chairman, and old friend of my parents, smiled warmly. After a whole variety of questions the secretary led me to the door. "We will be in touch with you very soon" he told me. Unknown to me a letter was sent to my father which he later gave me. It had pleased him greatly. "My dear Harry," it read. "We have just interviewed your daughter with a view to possible candidature of the L.C.C. I must tell you that she did extremely well. She combines your warmth, gleeful sense of humour and quick-witted impishness, with her mother's looks and dignity. It will be fun to have another Brittain in politics. I hear she is a much sought after speaker. Jolly good luck to her."

I sent a note to John Cartland thanking him for the Ashridge recommendation and giving him my news.

CHAPTER TWENTY-SEVEN

As we approached the third anniversary of President Roosevelt's death, a very fine bronze statue of the late president was about to be unveiled by Mrs. Eleanor Roosevelt in Grosvenor Square. To make clear my father's part in this wonderful ceremony, I need to return very temporarily to the summer of 1946. He and I were walking together over the little bridge spanning the lake in St. James's Park, just after I had been demobilised from the A.T.S. Stopping under the fig tree to admire the ducks, I remarked, "How lucky that this beautiful lake remained untouched, unlike 1915, when I can just recall that hideous empty area later to be filled with government offices." My father looked surprised. "Good gracious!" he commented. "I had absolutely forgotten that, but of course I spent most of the 'First War' years in the United States."

One or two curious swans swam towards us as we gazed in silence at the charming view. "Wouldn't it be splendid," my father burst out, "If this country would erect a memorial statue to President Roosevelt?" "Well, why not?" I added. My father straightened his shoulders as if coming out of a trance. "Why not?" he exclaimed, "Why not indeed?"

A man of lightning decision once a good idea had pierced his mind, he telephoned Lord Derby, the president of the Anglo-American Pilgrims', the organisation he had himself founded, to suggest the idea. Lord Derby was entranced immediately forming "The Franklin Roosevelt Memorial Committee" with the indefatigable Sir Campbell Stuart as chairman. A national appeal was set in motion, gathering enough funds by November 1946 to enable the committee to approach the distinguished sculptor, Sir William Reid Dick, to undertake the project.

And now in April 1948, this particularly striking statue of green bronze had been completed awaiting the moving unveiling ceremony at which King George the Sixth and Queen Elizabeth were to be present. It was a matter of sadness to all concerned that Lord Derby himself had not lived long enough to be present in Grosvenor Square in the bright sunshine of this memorable spring morning.

On a specially constructed dais of royal blue and gold, with a flower-bedecked rail of white lilac and crimson tulips under a pale green awning were seated Queen Mary, Princess Elizabeth with her new husband the Duke of Edinburgh, the young Princess Margaret, together with Mrs. Eleanor Roosevelt and Mr. and Mrs. Winston Churchill. The Queen sat in the very front with Dr. Fisher, the then Archbishop of Canterbury, Mr. Attlee the Prime Minister, and Major Harry Hooker, President Truman's personal representative.

Two fountains had been installed at either end of a flawless carpet of grass flanked with daffodils, narcissi and hyacinths, while the statue had been draped with the combined flags of Great Britain and the U.S.A. The flags of both countries also fluttered from twelve surrounding masts.

On a much smaller dais sat the American Ambassador with the committee of the Pilgrims and the leading government ministers. I had been given the honour of a place with this august assembly in view of my father's unique position.

Thousands lined the surrounding streets to watch this ceremony and in a specially constructed box one could just see the broad shoulders of Mr. Richard Dimbleby whose task it was to broadcast the proceedings for the B.B.C.

The Archbishop of Canterbury had himself worked out the unusual service. After a prayer, the King was led forward to speak which he did in stirring simple phrases.

"We shall, as we look at it, renew our pledge to continue to share with the American people the ideals of peace and freedom for which President Roosevelt strove with such untiring faith." Mrs. Roosevelt then moved slowly across a walk of broad white stone pausing for a moment before releasing the cord which allowed the flags to drop in graceful folds. The statue of the late President, standing erect and cloaked, with just the hint of a stick, sprang out of the pedestal, looking across at the sparkling splashing fountains, the water glistening rainbow-tinged against the bright sky. It had been Mrs. Roosevelt's personal request that her husband's memorial statue should be of a standing and not of a seated figure, having herself suggested the cloak.

The Royal Marines struck up the opening chords of the "Star Spangled Banner" moving Mr. Churchill to tears. Many memories may have flooded his mind. Grosvenor Square had been the place of his own boyhood home, where his famous father, Lord Randolph Churchill had died.

The King then placed a wreath of spring flowers at the foot of the memorial, followed by Major Harry Hooker, and Lord Greenwood the chairman of the Pilgrims'.

The ceremony over, it was a particularly charming gesture on the part of the King to seek out, and to congratulate my father on "Your inspiring idea which has now borne fruit."

To conclude this most spectacular occasion, in the evening, the Pilgrims were host to Mrs. Eleanor Roosevelt at a banquet in the

Plate 15

H.M. King George the Sixth and Mrs. Eleanor Roosevelt leaving the memorial statue of American President Franklin Delano Roosevelt after the unveiling ceremony in Grosvenor Square.

Savoy Hotel. It was, in fact, a very restricted meal to conform to rationing regulations. The guests were offered a sparse three course menu of soup, chicken with decorative vegetables, and, breaking away from austerity, a sweet built in the style of "The White House" in a solid cream-imitation ice made from dried milk, around which floated peaches, a gift from a South African well-wisher. A generous American had presented the champagne, hock and burgundy.

In recognition of my father's part as the original founder, he had been invited to join the chairman in receiving the guests. The charming suggestion was then made, that, as a widower, his daughter might be invited to stand beside him. Accordingly, in view of this great honour, I had taken infinite trouble to find a dress. In the end, my excellent dressmaker remodelled an old pre-war evening dress of midnight blue velvet, adding collar and cuffs of Brussels lace, a long-ago gift from my godmother. To enhance my appearance, my father had presented me with a spray of "Sir Harry Brittain" carnations of hothouse origin, a flower of a glorious rich red, tinged with an edge of flame. The spray of flowers, delivered straight to the Savoy, was awaiting my arrival in the care of the hard-working secretary of the Pilgrims', Mrs. Ada Doyle. Pinning them to my shoulder the kindly lady remarked, "Oh! my dear, now all you need is a glass slipper and a fairy prince!"

Lord Greenwood and his wife, both very old friends, took up their position in the foyer while my father and I stood nearby. A crescendo of cheering from the Strand warned us that the first distinguished guests were about to arrive.

Her Royal Highness Princess Elizabeth wearing an exquisitely pretty dress of yellow ruched tulle, together with her handsome bridegroom in naval officer's uniform were ushered in. The young couple were representing King George the Sixth and Queen Elizabeth. Soon, even wilder cheers accompanied the entry of Mr. Churchill and his beautiful wife, enthusiastically clapped by the hall porter and many of the Savoy Hotel staff. Then one by one came all the great war leaders with deafening cheers for Field Marshal Viscount Montgomery, whose immense array of medals could hardly find the space on his spare frame.

Mr. Ernie Bevin caused much amusement. Grasping the distinguished Field Marshal by the arm, the Foreign Secretary declared, "What you need, me lad, is a chest *my* size. You've too lean a figure. You'll 'ave all them medals toppling off into yer soup!" To my father Mr. Bevin questioned, "Well, 'Arry, 'ow d'yer think of all this? It's a great occasion."

Meanwhile Dr. Fisher (later Lord Fisher of Lambeth) looking magnificent in clerical evening attire was busily entertaining Mrs. Roosevelt, the guest of honour, who wore a lovely silver and black dress with a small lace cape over her shoulders.

As we moved into the tightly packed dining-room I realised that I had been awarded the extreme honour of sitting between the friendly Archbishop (a family contact of some years) and the austere Field Marshal, "Monty" to so many. Both these two outstanding personalities proved to be in mischievously high spirits and I was amazed to discover that the great soldier possessed such a splendid sense of humour. Throughout the meal they chaffed one another relating a whole series of ridiculous stories, giving great amusement to Mr. Richard Dimbleby seated opposite, and to many others within earshot.

A few quips and sallies remain in my memory.

"Do you know, Field Marshal," commenced the Archbishop, "That when I first entered the Church I asked a young curate to call on a family whose baby I had promised to baptise. Unfortunately I had given him the wrong address and the door was opened by a bachelor. 'Sorry padré,' said the house owner, 'I don't belong to your abomination!'"

"Well, I'll tell you a story, Archbishop. When I was a little boy I was sent to Sunday school. Our class were asked 'Who was sorry when the prodigal son returned?'. My form-mate answered immediately, 'The fatted calf!'"

The Archbishop continued. "When I was a schoolmaster I overheard a conversation between two schoolboys who had both rather fancied themselves in the school play. The first asked his colleague, 'Well, did I fill the hall with my resonant voice?' The reply came back, 'Of course not, you fool, you emptied it!'"

Now it was the Field Marshal's turn. "Years ago I had a regimental sergeant major who had been detailed to give the recruits a lecture on Christianity. This is what he said: 'In Christianity, a man may have only one wife and that is called monotony!'"

The Archbishop had thought of another story. "Once there was a small hotel where few visitors of importance came to stay. A bishop had booked in for a night. The little boot-boy was instructed to carry up the bishop's morning tea, knock on the door with the words, 'The boy is here my lord'. What the little boy actually announced was, 'The Lord is here, my boy'." Hilarious laughter greeted this exchange.

By contrast the speeches were very solemn. In prefacing the toast to Mrs. Roosevelt, Lord Greenwood presented her with a four foot replica in bronze of the Grosvenor Square statue of her late husband which she accepted with a most gracious acknowledgment. Two telegrams were then read, one from the King, and one from President Truman. Mr. Attlee followed, making a most sombre speech, and finally Mr. Churchill who stressed, "We are all united here tonight in paying our tribute to that inspiring leader, President Franklin Roosevelt."

My father and I slipped out to stand once again in our distinguished positions beside the Pilgrims' chairman and his wife in order to say goodnight to this august assembly of the departing famous. Finally a very small group had remained in the foyer still exchanging old memories. Mrs. Roosevelt, Mr. and Mrs. Churchill, Sir Campbell Stuart, who had worked so diligently to bring about the success of the entire day, and Mr. Richard Dimbleby.

Mrs. Roosevelt questioned Mr. Churchill. "Can you remember that little verse that you used to quote to my husband which always made him laugh?" The old warrior's face puckered in a deep frown, then, like the sun's appearance from behind a cloud, his whole countenance lit up and he started to declaim

"I *could* say life is one unending stream of worries
And appear most intelligent and smart.
But I'm stuck like a dope
With that thing they call hope,
And I can't get it out of my heart!"

"Waaael," concluded Mrs. Roosevelt, in her inimitable American accent, "Isn't that juuust beeeutiful!"

It seemed to be a delightful winding up of a unique occasion.

CHAPTER TWENTY-EIGHT

Midsummer had come and gone. After a long and difficult meeting of school governors, now one of my Kensington duties, I was sitting by the Serpentine watching the shimmering water, green with reflected tree shadows. A slow drift of white cloud floated over the coloured flower borders now a mass of peach, apricot and mahogany shades. Two pigeons alighted with their ridiculous refrain "Take *two* vows—Daisy!"

I had been invited to present myself to the Dulwich Conservative Association with a view to possible selection as one of their L.C.C. candidates for the 1949 election. Alderman Robert Jenkins, their prospective parliamentary candidate, whom I had met on the Kensington Borough Council, had warned me that a short speech would be required. Accordingly, in the pleasant peace of Hyde Park I was struggling to find some appropriate words.

Many changes had been taking place in the political world. Mr. Attlee's Labour Government, faced with immense problems, had dealt strenuously with the final phases of transition to independence in India, Ceylon and Burma. There was to be the creation of a new separate state, Pakistan. Lord Mountbatten, the last Viceroy of India, had been called in to prove his great qualities of imagination and energetic action to surmount the intensely difficult administrative problems. It was said that the transfer of power now covered one sixth of the world's total population. At the same time, the establishment of a North Atlantic Treaty Organisation, comprising all the powers of the European Atlantic Seaboard, excluding Eire and Spain but including Italy, Greece and Turkey, in association with Canada and the U.S.A., was about to become the most comprehensive military alliance in British history.

In addition, there was to be a supreme headquarters of Allied Powers in Europe, to be known as S.H.A.P.E. set up in Paris. Mr. Churchill, still out of office, but not inactive, was taking the first step towards the creation of a Council of Europe at Strasbourg. Deeply shocked at the running down of the former British Empire in such haste, Mr. Churchill had proclaimed in Parliament, "It is with grief that I stand by watching the spectacle of the clattering down of great portions of the British Empire with all its glories. I see it as a calamity which bears the taint of smear and shame." Mr. Attlee replied crushingly, "Old men are often fifty years behind the times!"

In this summer of 1948 I was again honoured with an invitation to the Buckingham Palace Garden Party wearing the same dress which I had had re-made for the previous July. Clothes were still strictly rationed and this was noticeable in Queen Mary's long white knitted coat. "She made it herself!" pronounced a cheerful Duke of Gloucester to my father. Many women were indeed following Queen Mary's example by unpicking baby clothes, whose owners had long grown out of them, and re-knitting them into grown-up garments.

The King looked very frail, indeed many rumours were now circulating about his ill-health over which there was considerable anxiety. There was happier news, however, about his elder daughter, who was expecting her first baby in November. There were rumours, too, that Queen Mary had saved a number of clothing coupons to give to her granddaughter.

Mr. Churchill's plan of the eventual political unification of Europe was being discussed with some animation in the royal tea tent, receiving considerable approval by many guests.

Fulfilling the most enjoyable engagement the following evening I went as the guest of Sir Alfred Munnings to the Royal Academy to view some of Mr. Churchill's lively and colourful paintings. The great man himself was absent, but his wife, looking her usual gracious self, was receiving the guests. At the end of the evening she invited me to join her small party. We had quite a long talk about the Roosevelt statue. "What a brilliant idea that was!" she exclaimed. She then went on to remind me that she had stood with my mother at the passing out parade of the O.C.T.U. at Windsor in 1942 when her nineteen-year-old daughter Mary had been one of my fellow A.T.S. cadets. Mary, now married to the then Captain Christopher Soames (now Lord Soames) had just presented her parents with a grandson, Nicholas. "She is very well and happy," her mother told me. Turning to Lord Jessel on her other side she described the meeting in Holland which her distinguished husband had just attended. "In Europe they call Winston 'The Father of Victory'," she announced with pride.

The summer session for the Kensington Borough Council was ending. Before going into recess I was appointed a manager of a school for backward and disturbed girls in Hammersmith. This was to prove a strange experience. The surroundings were very pleasant, bright classrooms, small well-furnished airy dormitories, good food, and for all the girls, pretty clothes. Indeed, materially, the children appeared to be in excellent circumstances. The dedicated staff, however, told me that the work was most difficult. Some pupils were withdrawn, others vicious and unpredictable. A few were pin-swallowers, a ruse to be taken into hospital thus gaining sympathy and attention. Nearly all were from broken homes, or, in some cases, no home at all but just abandoned on church doorsteps. The headmistress seemed a most remarkable woman and I much admired her.

Before the month ran out, I was called before the Dulwich selection board at the Conservative offices in Grove Vale. Squeezed into the agent's office, I was amazed to see so many other potential candidates, many of whom were women. The agent, helpful and encouraging put us all at our ease. "Women candidates will be called in alphabetical order," he explained, "But men candidates will be called in reverse alphabetical order from 'Z' backwards." Under this arrangement I was the first to be called.

Inside the association headquarters a formidable number of "selectors" had gathered, among whom I spotted Alderman Robert Jenkins who had given me much kindly encouragement from Kensington. Eight minutes had been allowed for each candidate, first a series of questions and then a brief speech. With no way of telling whether or not one had pleased the meeting, I withdrew encouraged by Mr. Jenkins' friendly smile.

A day later came a letter from the agent. "We now have a short list of six and you are invited to appear again in a week's time. Privately, you are the only woman candidate to reach the final and if you can put up anything like as good a show for the next board there should not be any doubt as to the result."

Very encouraged, I spent the weekend at Hawarden Royal Air

Force Station where my brother was commandant. Most happily his wife had completely recovered her health and was about to accompany the children to the farm in Cornwall. I had visited both children in their respective schools in the course of the year. My niece had settled happily, but not my nephew. Unable to probe the secrets of a little boy's mind, all one could do was to give him the best day possible, in the circumstances.

Before the week was out, I was to find myself journeying again towards Dulwich. Out of the murky windows of the tram (long discontinued) rattling its way over the Thames, I perceived a rainbow arching the whole sky. In the lurid light of sun and shadow, the colours appeared sensationally bright; green, lilac, saffron, tangerine and crimson, shot with deep purple and blue. Was this a good sign that my little "rollerball" of good luck would once again find its way into the right groove, I wondered. Rainbows were happy omens.

The agent greeted me warmly, ushering me again into the same room, where, much to my surprise, I was greeted with a burst of clapping. On this occasion the questions were limited and the candidate invited to deliver an eight minute speech. Not knowing any of my rivals, all I could do at the end was smile and withdraw.

Late in the evening, my telephone rang. The caller was Alderman Jenkins speaking from Mr. Charles Pearce's house in Dulwich. "Warmest congratulations!" he said. "We thought you would like to know at once that you were voted top of the list. Your colleagues will be Mr. Charles Pearce, the sitting L.C.C. member who has given long years of service as a Dulwich councillor, and Mr. Ronald Hensman, a newcomer like yourself." Expressing my very real thanks I told him how much I appreciated all his help as well as his kindness in sending me the news straight away. Mr. Pearce added a few words. "You were unrivalled, really first class. Together with Mr. Hensman, the three of us should be able to put up a good campaign. We must all get together very soon." Thanking him too for his kindness I went to bed that night very relieved. I had found both boards a considerable strain.

CHAPTER TWENTY-NINE

With August half-flown I accompanied an old F.A.N.Y. friend (whose friendship I am glad to say has survived the years), to a course at Ashridge entitled "Britain in the post-war world". It was not too strenuous and we revelled in the garden walks with the sky as blue as larkspurs and the honeyed scent of sweetpeas and roses. When tired, we shaded under the magnificent oak, said to have been planted in the sixteen hundreds. From time to time, it called our attention to its majestic presence by scattering acorns.

At Kirklands, meanwhile, my father had reached the final stage of his book *Happy Pilgrimage* due to be published in the New Year. It happened that the trivial announcement of my success at Dulwich had found its way into the parish magazine. On reading this, L. went completely beserk. The doctor was summoned. After many difficulties L. was persuaded to enter a psychiatric hospital for voluntary treatment. On my return to my London flat the doctor telephoned, giving me the news.

"It was very commendable of your father to employ such a mentally sick woman," he said. "But very hard on you." I agreed. He continued, "She suffers from an overweening self-pity, characteristic of her mental affliction, her rage against you was, of course, pure jealousy, you had everything she lacked. Also she thought you had thwarted her ambition to marry your father which we all know was fantasy." I replied that I had felt sorry for her. "She seemed such an incredibly pathetic soul, locked in the prison of her own poisoned mind." "Well, I am glad you look at it that way," the doctor added. "I have advised your father not to become embroiled again and let us hope that the psychiatric specialists may be able to do something for her." I, too, hoped for the same result, also that she would never reappear in my life.

Resettled in London, I was now to find myself with an extraordinarily busy schedule. Letters reached me in dozens.

Requests had arrived from all the ward chairmen inviting me to speak at Dulwich functions. The Young Conservatives urged me to judge a speaking competition. The chairman of the women's branches clamoured for talks at afternoon gatherings. The agent sent a request for a series of articles on "Women in Local Government", and a newspaper called *The Londoner* also invited me to send a "potted biography" together with photographs, "several if you have them," they stressed. I was now to be kept extremely busy for many weeks.

Contacting my new fellow candidate, Mr. Ronald Hensman, we agreed to lunch together, when we could get to know each other. He had little spare time, occupying a senior position in Cable and Wireless. Mr. Pearce, a retired schoolmaster, was more easily available and I was soon to realise what very charming colleagues the good people of Dulwich had chosen when they did me the honour of selecting me as their candidate.

My army medals had now arrived, two solid discs, larger and heavier than the old half-crown, bound up with appropriate ribbons. Information was included as to where miniatures could be procured. Miniatures were much more convenient. Having now become a prospective L.C.C. candidate, although the official "adoption" had yet to take place, I was awarded a very small amount of petrol which was to prove a great boon.

With the coming of autumn my father sought my company at Kirklands and we went on picnics, treading our way through the golden rustling leaves. My future, he hoped, as a county councillor, had given him enormous pleasure. I never referred to the subject of L. It was enough that she had left. His typescript was in the hands of the publishers.

Autumn lingered, but in the Dulwich parks, and I was getting to know my way around the constituency area, leaves were drifting down, a glorious sight, yellow, rust and orange. Ronald Hensman and I had begun to work out our canvassing schedule. In the evenings, he and I met together, but in the afternoons I remained under the guidance of the convivial Mr. Pearce, a much older man, then in his early sixties. Ronald and I ended our canvassing evenings by having supper together in a pleasant little restaurant close to Victoria Station, long pulled down. Here we talked animatedly about our respective experiences and future plans.

Rumours that the King was now suffering from a circulation problem cast a certain shadow over the happy news that Princess Elizabeth had given birth to a son, the baby destined to become the future Prince of Wales. Other important news came from the U.S.A. where President Harry Truman had been elected President in his own right, contrary to expectations.

With the blue misty smoke rising from many bonfires, and in the shortening evenings, all potential L.C.C. candidates were called to weekly meetings in the building of the Girls' Friendly Society in Greycoat Place. Here we received excellent lectures on all the many subjects connected with council work. Mr. Henry Brooke, our leader (later Lord Brooke), was indefatigable, painstakingly pointing out the snares. He was ably backed up by other senior and experienced members of the L.C.C. as it was in those days.

It was not all work, however, and I enjoyed some remarkably good plays and musicals at weekend matinées. Especially lively were the fine companies from America; *Annie Get Your Gun* and *Oklahoma.* My dear actress friend, Miss Vera Beringer, often accompanied me.

In November I received news that my cousin Pamela, now Mrs. Manners, had been taken into Guy's Hospital. Fortunately, the operation she had been obliged to undertake had not been serious and I was allowed to see her. She now had two young children, a girl and a boy. Later I went to visit her in her pleasant flat in Blackheath. Her naval officer husband was then working at Greenwich. It was most enjoyable to hear news of her parents, who had always shown me so much kindness, and of her three sisters whose respective service husbands had been demobilised. On the Brittain side, my cousin Joan, now Mrs. Bennett, who had settled in South Africa, was soon to present her husband with a second son. Uncle Bob, delighted with his grandsons, sent me a number of charming family photographs. My cousin, Michael, had just passed his eighteenth birthday and was due to join the family business in Auckland.

At the beginning of December my colleagues and I were officially "adopted" as the prospective Conservative candidates for Dulwich. A little notice appeared in *The Times* leading to a most charming letter from Uncle Emile at Dundridge.

"Aunt Sybil and I wish you the very greatest success in your election contest. We think it is absolutely splendid the way you have decided to carry on the family political tradition. Don't fail to invite yourself to Dundridge whenever you feel in need of a break, we will always be delighted to see you. As you know, we have only the minimum of staff, two gardeners, one wife who helps occasionally with housework, otherwise no one. It is an incredibly changed world. Thank goodness our girls are happy in their marriages; we have a host of grandchildren. Felicitations to your father. I hear the new book will be published shortly. We look forward to reading it. Best of luck again and a most happy Christmas.''

Another very kind letter reached me from my dear old friend Sir Patrick Hannon.

"After your outstanding career in the women's service, I read that you are now prepared to accept the obligations of municipal government! I do wish you a triumphant success. It is indeed fitting that you should march in your wonderful mother's footsteps. Her contribution to the civic life of London as well as to the public life of the country will always remain a grateful memory to all who had the privilege of knowing her. Bless you, my dear child.''

I was in my mid-thirties, but was always to remain a "child" to this warm-hearted friend. He was, in fact, senior to my father.

I was to share that Christmas with my father who celebrated his seventy-fifth birthday on Christmas Eve. My brother, now south again from Hawarden, joined me in a dinner for a family reunion at our favourite restaurant in Soho called Gennaros. Our generous Uncle Bob had sent the family yet another food parcel, greatly appreciated by us all.

Rationing continued and "The New Look" as it was called, wide shoulders with small waists and enormously long skirts, gathered in thick folds, was causing fashion-conscious women some difficulty. Ingenious needlewomen combined two former garments with contrasting material and a "clothes hospital" sprang to life in Church Street. The lucky ones with enough coupons, took great advantage of the attractive bold new style. But it was to remain a "make do and mend" epoch for a few more years.

My friend, John Cartland, now married with two young children, invited me to a most enjoyable party on New Year's Eve. He was still working for the Oxford Appointments Board.

CHAPTER THIRTY

In the new year of 1949, the great Festival of Britain was being prepared. Planned for 1951, this festival was designed to show what Britain hoped to produce and sell in the future. Architects were to be given their first major opportunity since the war in designing a spectacular concert hall, later to become known as "Festival Hall". There were to be many other attractions including pleasure gardens. Battersea Park was due to be laid out as a fairground. Advertising, however, remained difficult as the press were suffering from strict rationing of newsprint.

The local authorities, still living in sombre times, were now struggling to meet the urgent requirements of housing, and a whole crop of strange little dwellings, known as prefabricated dwellings had appeared, some quite cosy, since the end of the war. In addition the councils were starting to build giant blocks of flats, many on the bombed out areas which were not proving as popular as had been hoped. In the West End the one-time aristocracy, now almost vanished, unable to keep up their pre-war houses, had sold them for flats. Many offices had come into existence in the one-time graceful squares of former purely residential houses. London looked very shabby and untidy.

In the outside world, Russia was tightening her grip on Eastern Europe. The Communists announced that because the West had set up an independent German Government under Chancellor Adenauer, the Eastern Zone was now to become known as the German Democratic Republic. A successful revolt had taken place by Marshal Tito in Yugoslavia leading to cruel purges among the other satellite states.

For those of us now plodding around the streets, hopefully seeking the votes of our supporters for the council election, it was fortunate that the winter of 1949 was reasonably mild. Frequently, however, the clouds were hanging low and iron-grey racing along with rain spilling out as if being squeezed by giant tongs, harnessed in space. In Dulwich there were endless lines of small dwellings, with here and there, a six storey building and an occasional lofty mansion. The great tower blocks of high rise flats were still under construction. Much of Dulwich remained very agreeable, no longer the green meadows and pink-blossomed orchards of earlier times, but still with the feeling of a country village. Towards the Peckham side many streets became narrow and grey.

Our election posters were gradually making an appearance in occasional windows and it was a shock to see one's own photograph peering through the curtains. Most householders greeted me kindly, almost all politely, and a few with genuine enthusiasm. I had already achieved the title of "Luv" to a great number.

"You'll be all right here, luv," one lady told me. "Me and all my family's always voted Conservatory."

Some strange problems were raised. One elector pressed me to see if I could sell her piano. Another asked if I could get her son's painting exhibited in the Royal Academy, and a third wanted to find a home for her daughter's canary. It might not have been a whirlpool of life but I found it most informative and interesting.

My talks to the women members in their afternoon meetings were continuing and it was gratifying to find the halls becoming more and more crowded.

At the end of January, the Spelthorne women's branch invited me to speak on any subject of my choice at their evening annual general meeting. Alighting at Staines station I was met by the charming chairman who informed me that their prospective parliamentary candidate, a Mr. Craddock, would be conducting the meeting. I had chosen the subject "Conservative Principles" which I could now back with my knowledge of the country's constitution gained from my many talks to the A.T.S.

In an extremely well attended gathering I found I was being listened to with rapt attention. When the lights failed, some far-sighted member produced a candle, much to the concern of Mr. Craddock who felt I might need to read notes. Happily, knowing the subject so thoroughly, I remained unconcerned.

At the end the clapping was so enthusiastic that I felt I had certainly lit a spark in this particularly alert audience. Later, over coffee and sandwiches, congratulations were almost embarrassing but pleasant to hear.

Outside the hall, in the sharp air of a January night with black velvet sky and a million dancing stars, Mr. Craddock offered me a lift back to London in his car. I accepted gratefully. "If I may say so," he began as the car gained speed, "That was a brilliant speech. I have never heard the case for Conservatism so succinctly expressed, and your knowledge of history is remarkable. Where did you learn it all?" I described my experiences as an A.T.S. education staff officer. "You carried on without a flicker when the lights failed." "Well, that was easy, I knew the subject so well." Mr. Craddock continued, "I am secretary of the Parliamentary Candidates Association and I am determined to put your name forward. Will you allow that?" I felt obliged to give my consent.

As everyone loves flattery, perhaps I may be forgiven for quoting the felicitous letter I received from the Spelthorne branch secretary.

"Thank-you indeed for coming to speak at our meeting. Your speech was quite enthralling. We all enjoyed it immensely and members are still talking about you. You really captured our hearts. If all women speakers had your gift there would be no men members in Parliament! We are still wondering where you gathered, and even more remarkable, how you retain all your historical knowledge. We do wish you all possible success in your fight for the L.C.C. at Dulwich. Many members would like to come and canvass for you." It was certainly most uplifting to feel that one had been so much appreciated.

In early February, a weekend course had been arranged at the Grand Hotel, Eastbourne, on local government. All candidates had received an invitation for what was to prove a most enjoyable occasion. Ronald and I travelled together to find a sea calm, a sparkling blueish-silver, with white-lipped wavelets crossing over each other in confusion breaking into wisps of coloured spray. There was still enough light to enable us to walk along the sands, noisy with quarrelling seagulls.

The course had been planned in four sections, housing, education, health and finance, interspersed with discussion groups. On the Saturday night the hotel ran a dance. My friend John Cartland, staying a night with his mother, telephoned to ask if he might join the Dulwich party for the dance. Circling round to the lively music he opened the conversation at once. "Look, I've heard from Craddock. He thinks as I do that you're the ideal woman candidate. You are way out ahead now on the right side of the track, all you need to do is to pick up the challenge.''

Looking out of my bedroom window later over the sea, a monster moon had come up like a giant cheese. I thought of the recent conversation on the dance floor. Quite apart from the financial stringency I really had no ambition to enter Parliament. My father was right in his assertion that it was "All kicks and no thanks''. I could remember quite enough of his life to know the truth of that phrase!

John came to Eastbourne station to see us off. "Well, don't forget,'' he urged. "As soon as you plunge into the wider political seas I will be the first to wish you 'bon voyage'.'' I would have been utterly horrified if I could have read his personal future. He was to be brutally murdered on a holiday in France with the son, of whom he was so proud, falling under suspicion. It still remains an unsolved and apparently completely motiveless murder in the French criminal records. I still grieve for his widow and the family at the loss of so pleasant a man.

On 27th February my brother celebrated his fortieth birthday. After lunching together he took me to visit the Rootes' showrooms to see a replica of the handsome Hillman Minx car which was shortly to be delivered to him. With few exceptions, these cars were destined for export only. It was now that my brother took me into his confidence. A new post as air attaché in Rumania was likely to come to him some time later in the year. All seemed to be going well with the family and the farm in Cornwall appeared to be progressing very favourably.

Now I heard from the Kensington Borough Council that I had been selected again for the Brompton ward. The election date had been fixed for 12th May. If luck stayed with me there was a prospect that I might again be returned unopposed.

CHAPTER THIRTY-ONE

The trial of the war criminals, better known as the Nuremburg trials, had now ended. There had been remarkably little public interest. In my many weeks of canvassing in Dulwich, I never came across excessive bitterness against Germany. The feeling of revenge, as expressed in the sayings "Hang the Kaiser!" and "Make Germany pay!" so prevalent in 1918 were non-existent.

The electors' desires were simple. A little more food, although Lord Woolton's fair rationing had been widely praised; soap off the ration; the availability of new kettles and kitchen pans, and particularly the opportunity to replace sheets and blankets now worn almost threadbare in many homes. There seemed to be an amazing kindliness and tolerance among the voters some even expressing approval of the self-sacrifice the country had been obliged to shoulder in order to win the war. They were indeed the true representatives of Mr. Churchill's bulldog breed.

We had now reached March, and with the L.C.C. election date arranged for 7th April, the time had come to undergo the ordeal of public meetings. My colleagues and I appeared in a number of halls in different parts of the constituency. On the whole our meetings went well, although sparsely attended. The great difficulty for us all was in trying to find something fresh to say. Throughout the previous autumn and winter we had all attended dances, school plays, Christmas bazaars, ward annual dinners, women's branch jumble sales, Young Conservatives' galas, speaking competitions, school prizegivings, even a party given by the Salvation Army. Our joint "repertoire" was wearing thin! So tired, in fact, was poor Mr. Robert Jenkins, that he addressed his remarks to "Mr. Chairman" when he himself was in the chair.

Keen to show his support, and perhaps to experience the fun of an election campaign after many years, my father offered to drive me to all the wards and polling stations on our election day which had dawned very wet and chilly. We lunched at the Half Moon Hotel, where my colleagues had gathered. Wonderful supporters had rallied and there was a great deal of final door-knocking and driving voters to the polling stations although petrol was still rationed. I much appreciated this warm support. Earlier in the campaign an immense number of good people had come forward to help with the dreary job of stuffing and addressing envelopes and pushing leaflets through letter-boxes. When I expressed my thanks to the women's branches I was touched to receive the reply "You have struck a chord in this constituency and we all wish you a great future."

By late afternoon, my father, then in his 76th year, was looking tired. Thanking him most warmly, I suggested that he should now go home to his flat. Ronald and I then joined forces doing what little we could until darkness when we went to find a meal outside the Dulwich area hoping not to be recognised.

At 9.00 p.m. there was to be a meeting in the committee rooms where our helpers, together with the hard-working "tellers" had gathered to give their reports. Our count was not due to take place until the following morning. I was losing my voice having spent so much of the day shaking hands and expressing my endlessly repeated thanks, so I gratefully accepted the inevitable cup of tea which the agent handed me. "As you know," he repeated, "The count is to be held at the Mary Datchelor Girls' School. Be prepared for a long wait, it may be a close-run thing. No need to be too early, come about 10.30 and have a good rest tonight. It was splendid to see Sir Harry here," he wound up.

The hall porter at Kensington Close, a staunch Conservative, had saved me a number of newspapers the following morning. As he handed them to me I could tell by his smile that the news was encouraging. In the constituencies where counts had been completed there had been a surprising number of Conservative gains. "Good luck, Miss," he said. "When you come back later I hope I shall be addressing you as councillor."

Catching my usual tram from Victoria, I looked out on a dull misty day, and with a humid air. London looked steel-grey with so many ancient rain-washed buildings. It took some while for the tram to reach Camberwell Green so I settled down to study the newspapers.

Inside the girls' school hall, the children having broken up for Easter holidays, tables and benches stretched right round the room. Scores of volunteers, both men and women, were handling tiny little bundles of votes with checkers standing behind them. In the centre of the room, both with completely expressionless faces, stood the two respective party agents. No Liberal candidates had contested the Dulwich seat. Many women supporters beckoned me to join them which I did gratefully. My two colleagues, together with the Socialist candidates, preferred to keep on the move.

As the agent had warned, it was to be an immensely long wait. At length, Mr. Jenkins touched my arm. "Well done, I think you're safely in, you may be top of the poll." Ronald approached from behind with his thumbs up. "It's in the bag, we are far ahead, they can't catch us now." I was swept by an enormous feeling of relief. Our efforts had paid off.

Figures were being scratched on paper. After some whispered conversations the agent approached me. "Heartiest congratulations you were a hot favourite, a magnificent result!" A borough council official then stepped forward and asked for silence, declaring that it was his duty to announce the figures:

A. G. R. Brittain	16,128	Conservative
R. H. Hensman	16,000	Conservative
C. Pearce	15,558	Conservative
A. Crossman	13,410	Labour
H. F. Lennard	12,529	Labour
M. F. Lucas	12,346	Labour

The announcement was greeted with a great surge of clapping and cheering from our side while Mr. Pearce voiced our joint thanks to all officials and volunteers. Then there was an enormous amount of thanking and handshaking all round. It was certainly a most exhilarating experience.

The final London result was announced at 6.00 p.m. It was a draw, 64-64 with the one and only L.C.C. Liberal, Sir Percy Harris, holding the balance to make up the 129 seats allotted to the London County Council at that time.

My father gave me a celebratory dinner at the Carlton Club (Ladies' Side). Our old family friend, Sir Montague Barlow joined us. "Not for nothing did I carry this victorious political lady to safety in the First World War," he declared, referring to his kindness in coming to keep an eye on the family at the time of my father's absence in America in the period 1915-1917. (When the Zeppelin raids started it was thought that the building next door would be safer than our own Georgian house in Cowley Street. Being about five years old at the time, Sir Montague had carried me from my cot wrapped in blankets.) Others then joined us and cheerfully drank my health in a specially ordered bottle of wine. "Your Dad's thrilled to death," one of them told me.

My post the following morning was overwhelming. Telegrams and letters poured in from so many kind relations and friends. The hall porter was delighted. "Councillor, you will need a postman to yourself if this goes on!" he jested. Soon my arm ached from writing all the letters of thanks but it was very heart-warming. I went out to buy great bunches of flowers to send to the agent's wife and to all the wonderful ward chairmen and their wives who had allowed their homes to be disrupted for so many weeks. Much later, I gave a special thank-you party in Kensington Close to everyone concerned. My finances were running very low and I was deeply appreciative of the generous cheque my father then put into my account.

The onus of acting as the casting vote was not to remain on Sir Percy Harris for very long. Holding a larger number of Aldermanic seats, the Socialists were able to claim themselves as winners. It was a great disappointment.

Shortly we were all to take our seats in the council chamber. Dame Barrie Lambert, a very old friend of my mother took my arm. "How lovely to greet you here and you are so like your mother. Wouldn't she have been delighted?" Another very kind friend of earlier days took me under her wing. She was Mrs. Norah Runge and I had always been an admirer. She had telephoned me words of encouragement more than once during the election campaign. Now she escorted me on a conducted tour of the County Hall buildings which seemed a veritable maze of twisting passages. "What fun to have you here," she told me, "And with all the prestige of being top of the poll." "I think that was pure luck," I responded. "Oh! Not at all," came the answer. "Several people told me you had a winning smile worth any number of votes!"

CHAPTER THIRTY-TWO

Easter had now arrived. On Maundy Thursday, taking up the extremely kind invitation to Dundridge, I jumped out of the train at Totnes. Uncle Emile met me and we drove along the familiar road with the red earth almost pink-tinged in the soft light of an April evening. The newly-leafed emerald-green trees appeared to be holding out their arms as if in greeting while the balmy air blew gently from the south-west. Aunt Sybil led me to my room packed with spring flowers. Only one other guest had arrived, Mrs. Eva Lockett, widow of Aunt Sybil's brother. All gave me the warmest of welcomes.

Helping Eva pick primroses, violets and daffodils for Gerry and her husband, due to arrive on Good Friday, she confided to me, "Our dear couple were so thrilled with your election triumph. They are both so proud of you and so delighted that you are keeping up the election tradition. They hope you will go into Parliament." Late in the evening, Gerry and her husband arrived, together with baby daughter, a friendly spaniel, and a very nervous Siamese cat called "Mistletoe".

It was very strange to find Dundridge entirely without staff. Aunt Sybil had developed into a remarkably competent cook and we all helped with the household affairs. On Easter Sunday Eva offered to baby-sit, so we all went together to St. Andrew's Church, Harberton, sitting in the Harvey pew. Later I accompanied Uncle Emile on a walk, taking many dogs. "Do you miss the old days?" I asked him. "It's a tremendous struggle for Aunt Sybil, but as long as we can manage, we hope to hold on. It will be a great wrench to let the old place go, but obviously we will be bound to have to face it one day." I commiserated. He went on, "It's a relief that the girls have made good marriages."

After receiving most generous Easter hospitality from the older generation, it was now my turn to look after my own niece and nephew on the unpopular day of returning to school. Delivered early to my flat, off their Cornish train, we spent the morning at the Natural History and Science Museums before the best lunch I could acquire for them. Poor David began to look more and more morose as we reached Paddington where he was to blend with a whole throng of small boys dressed in similar clothes. All I could do was to treat him to magazines of his choice, some bars of nuts and raisins (unrationed), and some additional pocket money, before handing him over to a pleasant-looking young master. In no time this efficient young man had organised his charges into a group, clambering in the most disciplined manner into the train. Various mothers, older sisters, or possibly aunts, stood and waved as the train drew away.

My niece, luckier than her brother, having a day in hand (as these trains never synchronised), asked if she could be taken to see Madame Tussauds. An energetic and vivacious twelve-year-old, she added greatly to the amusement of other visitors particularly on a staircase, where she gave a shriek of surprise. It appeared that an attendant, whom she had supposed to be made of wax, had winked at her. When we were faced by the grotesque reflections of ourselves in the distorting mirrors she laughed with such delighted hilarity that others joined in. Finally, we sought a Devonshire cream tea, as it was called, in a little restaurant named "The Dutch Oven" before I handed her over to her friend in Manchester Square, where she was to stay the night. There were times when being a maiden aunt appeared to be more exhausting than political canvassing!

In Kensington Gardens, an exquisite shell-pink magnolia had burst into flower. It was time to pay attention to the election for the Kensington Borough Council. Very happily for me, no opponent had come forward for the Brompton Ward and I was again returned unopposed. This was a most delectable ward comprising the Albert Hall, the Brompton Oratory and a number of edifying museums. I felt honoured to keep it to myself.

The council, now newly elected, was also to be honoured by being known as the Royal Borough of Kensington from mid-1949 onwards. We also received further exciting news that Mr. Churchill had consented to accept the "Freedom of the Borough" in a specially prepared ceremony at the beginning of June. It thus

followed that a few days later on a showery morning, with
hundreds lining the rain-soaked pavements, Mr. Churchill and his
wife arrived at the Town Hall. A gigantic ovation awaited them.
The mayor opened the proceedings against prolonged and almost
deafening applause while the great statesman signed the Freeman's
Roll. He was then to receive a baton, containing a scroll, an exact
replica of a scroll formerly carried by his great ancestor the Duke of
Marlborough. The mayor explained that the scroll had been cut
from a tree growing on the former battlefield at Blenheim. The
ceremony continued with one of Mr. Churchill's unique speeches
bringing members to their feet singing the well-known refrain "For
he's a jolly good fellow" which was taken up spontaneously by the
crowd outside. The charming ceremony was followed by a lunch,
given by the mayor, at the De Vere Hotel, where a number of Mr.
Churchill's family were awaiting him, including his son Randolph,

Plate 16

*Tea on Dundridge verandah—my uncle and aunt, Sir
Samuel and Lady Harvey, widely popular, hard-
working public figures: unsparingly generous hosts to
the family.*

recently married to his second bride, the former Miss June Osborne.

Duly settled in the hotel foyer, out of the rain, the baton was passed round to the council members. It had been secured in a handsome brown leather case with a red lining embossed with initials. We all found its weight most imposing. In her place next to the mayor, Mrs. Churchill, smiling as I passed, whispered to me, "Mary is expecting another baby. We would love it if Nicholas could have a sister." The only Churchill grandson, known as young Winston, was away at school. Julian Sandys, the eldest grandson, was also at school. There were, however, daughters and granddaughters at this happy occasion.

A few days later Mr. Harold Macmillan gave a most interesting talk at the Town Hall. At that time his name had not come forward as a prospective Prime Minister. No one expected that Mr. Anthony Eden (later Lord Avon), the obvious successor to Mr. Churchill, would retire in the prime of life. The Suez tragedy was some years in the future.

I was now beginning to find my way around County Hall and had been much intrigued with the council undertakings. Mr. Brooke, our hard-working political leader on the opposition front bench had warned us that we might have to undergo the strain of two all-night sittings discussing the financial estimates. These two nights, separated by a fortnight, were quite memorable, not for the speeches, but for the extremely interesting conversations with colleagues in the coffee-and-sandwich intervals with which we regaled ourselves. In those long-ago days, despite the post-war shabbiness of England's cities, it was a happier time. There were no punks, rockers, mods, skinheads, rastafarians, pornshops or muggers. Old ladies and young girls could walk safely in the streets. There was still, for want of a better phrase, a respect for decency. Rent-a-mob was unheard of.

CHAPTER THIRTY-THREE

There now followed an extremely busy summer. The days whirled by in a succession of council meetings, committee meetings—I was now a member of the L.C.C. Education Committee—school boards, school management and continuous speeches to both afternoon and evening meetings.

In June the London Conservative Union gave a party on the terrace of the House of Commons and we were treated to that rarest of delights in the still-rationed years, strawberries and cream with enough sugar to sweeten.

Aunt Winnie arrived in London for my birthday and my father took us both to Pruniers for a delightful dinner. I was able to act as hostess to Aunt Winnie at County Hall in which she appeared to be most interested. I also gave a cocktail party at Kensington Close in the newly-opened Edinburgh Room, a pleasant way of thanking my many kind friends.

A picture remains in my mind of tea on the terrace of County Hall overlooking the Thames with my many clever colleagues. It was thought that King George the Sixth, that most upright and respected of monarchs, was now seriously affected by circulation problems. Should his daughter accede to the throne, we mused, would we enter another golden age of prosperity and peace, or if we did, would the flowers of affluence fade? The hootings of Thames barges were loud, but the sounds of the future could not be heard. We were to hold many conversations of this sort, but even the most far-seeing could not perceive the coming troubles of the decades ahead, immigration, inflation, strikes, high taxation, costly nationalised industries carefully shielded from competition, decreasing production and inadequate exports. These disturbing symptoms were far in the future on those sun-filled afternoons.

Arranging a glorious bunch of flowers one Sunday evening in July, brought back from Kirklands, I was interrupted by my telephone bell. The caller was Sir Herbert Williams.

"Will you do me a great kindness?" he asked. "There is to be a Primrose League afternoon meeting in Croydon where I have been billed to speak, but I have to sit on a Parliamentary Commission and will not be free. Will you it take for me? Craddock tells me you held his women's branch spellbound."

"Well, I'll certainly do my best," I responded.

"That's wonderfully kind of you, my wife would like you to lunch and then the chairman will escort you both to the meeting."

Dame Fortune smiled again as I delivered the promised talk to the Croydon Primrose League and I found this particular audience as enthusiastic as the one in the constituency of Spelthorne. So kind were the flattering remarks in the tea room afterwards that I found £1 notes being pressed into my hands for "the Party Funds". "You will never have a nicer compliment than that!" Lady Williams remarked.

Late that evening, Sir Herbert telephoned again. "I can't thank you enough," he said. "My wife tells me you electrified them! Now is there something I can do for you?" "I owe you a considerable debt already," I answered. "But for you I might never have had a shot at the L.C.C. but what I really need now is a bigger flat. Only a more sugar-coated future is likely to produce that!"

The Festival of Britain 1951 showing Skylon and Dome of Discovery.   *Plate 17*

He replied quite seriously, "But I think I can help you if you won't mind living in Bloomsbury. The chairman of the Foundling Estate Properties is a very old friend. There are certain flats put aside to accommodate professional single people. I'll get the secretary to ring you." It sounded too good to be true.

The secretary of the Foundling Estate Properties did indeed telephone the very next morning with the instructions, "Will you go along to our head office in Grenville Street, Brunswick Square, and ask for the manager, he should be able to suit you." Feeling quite excited I made an immediate appointment with the manager. The following morning he led me to a converted Georgian house, shabby on the outside but comfortable inside, in Lansdowne Terrace. No. 14 was about to be vacated. This flat possessed high ceilings, fine Georgian windows, and a most attractive view overlooking the green open space of Coram's Fields, with splendid lofty plane trees in full leaf. There were two spacious unfurnished rooms with kitchen and bathroom.

"If you would like it," said the manager, "You must make up your mind straight away as I have a long waiting list." In that summer of 1949 the opportunity was not likely to recur so I assented immediately. "Good," continued the manager. "Then come back to my office and we will go into details."

My father came along to view the flat, expressing approval. I collected my brother, too, after a most enjoyable lunch with him at the Bath Club. His appointment as air attaché in Bucharest was now definite. Lansdowne Terrace, together with so many other London streets had been knocked about by bombs, it would almost certainly be due for demolition in due course, but my brother agreed that, once one had secured a foothold, the company might be in a position to offer something better at a later date. Furnishing the flat was likely to become a challenge for my meagre funds, but a request for a series of articles entitled "First impressions of a Councillor" coming from Fleet Street helped greatly to embellish my finances. By August I was in residence. My first guest was my friend Joan W. whose kindness had enabled me to secure my independence in London so quickly after my A.T.S. demobilisation. Pleasant as Bloomsbury was, it had been a wrench to leave Kensington. One advantage gained was the rapid journey to County Hall. I now took a squat little tram (long vanished) which dived underground at Southampton Row emerging on the Embankment. My father was also one of my first visitors bringing along a greatly appreciated housewarming cheque to offset my many expenses.

For the third year running I was given the privileged invitation to attend the Buckingham Palace Garden Party, and this summer there were to be many questions about the forthcoming Festival of Britain rapidly gaining momentum.

The L.C.C. had celebrated its diamond jubilee at the end of July entertaining the beautiful young Princess Elizabeth dressed in shimmering white, accompanied by the handsome Duke of Edinburgh, while the whole river frontage had been floodlit. With inside passages and staircases banked with flowers, and the terrace a mass of fairy lights the building had been transformed. To add to the gaiety, the London Fire Brigade, ensconced on the river, had shot coloured plumes of spray into the water. To a London hot and sultry, this attractive river front had been a welcome sight. "Rubbing shoulders with history," my colleague Ronald Hensman announced. My other colleague, Mr. Charles Pearce, had had the honour of being appointed deputy chairman.

With the ending of July all council activities went into recess and the rest was welcome, but there was soon to be renewed political activity in Dulwich for the Conservative parliamentary candidate, Mr. Robert Jenkins. The Labour Government was entering its fifth year.

Plate 18

With my twelve-week-old nephew, David, a month before the eruption of World War Two.

CHAPTER THIRTY-FOUR

The summer wound on. As the August shadows stirred under flickering sunlight and the crouching clouds gave way to vivid patches of blue, I explored the pleasant grounds of the college in Yorkshire, called Swinton, recently donated to the Conservative Party. I had undertaken to spend a fortnight in these impressive surroundings where, in the peaceful country scene the air felt sweet and pure. After the oppressive heat and exhaustion of a busy summer the change was enlivening.

My fellow students and I were to undergo a course entitled "Whither Britain in the second half of the twentieth century?" We had a number of excellent lecturers on foreign affairs, and heard that President Truman had now authorised the manufacture of the "H" bomb, a nuclear weapon of unimaginable destructive power. Home politics were much discussed. The Labour Government having made immense changes along the road to nationalisation together with the establishment of a welfare state (already called the parasite state), had also procured independence for India, Pakistan, Burma and Ceylon. Many now felt that all-embracing state control was growing alarmingly and that nationalisation would require ever increasing subsidies from the taxpayer.

On my return, my father had expressed a wish to visit the sea, so I accompanied him to Charmouth where we stopped in a charming inn called "The Coach and Horses". It was wet and windy and gusts of wind seemed to be tearing up whole mouthfuls of sea hurling it back against the sand. We did, however, manage to have a dip or two which felt adequately bracing. In the fields, the newly collected hay leaned heavily as if in need of support. Petrol was too scarce for long car journeys.

Back in the benevolent countryside of Hampshire, with the butter-coloured corn now safely gathered, I was to spend a further week's holiday with my father before returning to my new flat in

Bloomsbury. Here my brother stayed for a few days, his capable hands rendering me great service by the erection of shelves and the sorting of electrical problems. I would have been disappointed could I have foreseen that his imminent posting to Rumania would cause him to be absent from my wedding in a year's time; but happily I had not been gifted with clairvoyant powers.

Aunt Winnie had now arrived in the Russell Hotel on her way to Sicily to join a British Legion party on the sad journey to see her son's grave. She was very nervous as the party was booked to travel by air, never before experienced. My brother played a splendid part in reassuring her. Welcoming her a few days later on her return I was able to persuade her to accompany me to one or two theatre visits to lift her mind from her sadness.

In late September work began again in earnest and I joined my L.C.C. colleagues for the weekly "surgeries" as they were called, a means of trying to help solve our constituents' many problems. Nearly all of these related to housing, or more accurately the lack of housing. All that could be offered to begin with was to add the names to a waiting list already of immense length. We found it a tragic situation.

Soon we were to attend the ceremony of the laying of the foundation stone for the new concert hall to be known as Festival Hall. This was carried out by the Prime Minister, appropriately supported by the chairman of the L.C.C. Against the background of the river traffic and the bustle and rumble of London it was to prove a memorable occasion.

The kind women's branches of Dulwich had invited me to be their guest of honour at a lunch to be held in a local hotel necessitating an entirely new speech. Accordingly, after a meeting of the Kensington Libraries Committee, I rested in Kensington Gardens one October morning to work out a speech I was to call "London in the shadow of history". It was conker time again, soon to be followed by the gold and lemon-yellow of the autumn scene with the magenta dahlias glowing as if almost luminous. At the end of the lunch I was presented with a glorious bouquet of flowers from the branch chairman collected and put together from their own personal gardens, a compliment I greatly appreciated.

I had now been requested to become a governor of a school in Wimbledon for blind children. I found this a saddening experience, although the children, to whom this was a natural world, appeared to flourish under the care of a most devoted and dedicated staff. I was shown a kind of netball game in the school playground where the children followed a ball constructed around a jingling bell, tinkling in a different sound when handled.

The Dulwich schools took great note of harvest festival time, inviting us all to participate in some of the services. These were frequently followed by plays produced and acted by the children without adult help, some of which were to prove perfect little gems.

It was now our duty to entertain hosts of young schoolchildren in County Hall, causing the austere building to ring with enthusiastic young voices. We had to dig deeply into our private pockets to provide them with adequate teas!

The Conservative conference was now taking place at the Empress Hall, Earls Court, with Mr. Churchill billed to speak on the subject close to his heart "The Charter of the United Nations". As a great historian, the former Prime Minister's knowledge was thought to stretch well back into European history. His unique prestige and dynamic eloquence at the head of this great new movement had caused exceptional interest. As council members we were among the privileged to be given tickets. The speech Mr. Churchill gave that night proved to be scintillating. Perhaps history will one day show the great worth of the original idea of a United Europe when the quarrels about butter mountains, wine lakes, lamb exports, apples or turkeys will have been forgotten.

As the great statesman struggled his way through the crowd to get to his car, the police fought frantically to clear a passage. Mobs of enthusiastic citizens surged forward in an effort to grasp his hand. The ovation and applause had been so deafening that even in his remarkable experience, it could hardly have been surpassed. Many said that Mr. Churchill's fervent desire to create a Council of Europe would one day lead to an effective West European Federal Union. Perhaps it is Europe's misfortune that this did not follow.

We were on the waning tide of the year 1949 with gales snatching the lingering leaves, many still aglow with their painted tints, the fires of autumn not yet extinguished. Few bright days remained, but on one of these I was to repeat my talk on "London in the shadow of history" to the Conservative members of West Dulwich. The setting sun, pale ochre, disappeared into a violet haze.

CHAPTER THIRTY-FIVE

It was in a County Hall debate, touching on the misfortune of illiterate children that I was to make my "maiden speech" a few days later. Fellow members made remarkably kind and congratulatory remarks, particularly Sir Percy Harris, the only Liberal, and one of the older members. "Simply first class," he exclaimed, gripping my hand. "You have the ideal voice and you put your points over superbly. But I shall have to write to your dad to tell him that you have made an old fogey like me look really past it!" Our Conservative leader, Mr. Brooke, sent me a delightful note. "Your speech made a great impression," he wrote, "Not only splendidly audible but presented with much charm. Warmest congratulations and thanks." Even the chairman came forward with kind words. "A brilliant 'maiden speech', you should have a great council future. All our side were riveted!"

Now I had to dash back to Kensington where there was to be a children's book week. A book lover myself from early years, I had worked enthusiastically for this exhibition. Happily it was to prove a gratifying success. Television, revived from pre-war days, had restarted regular transmissions from Alexandra Palace, but the great boom starting about the early 1950s had yet to spread. Only a very limited number of the now ubiquitous television aerials could then be seen. The viewing habit was to spread with unbelievable rapidity in the next few years. At that time, however, books were greatly treasured.

The tear-off calendar, having reached December, soon became a reminder that Christmas was approaching. In Trafalgar Square for the second year, a gift Christmas tree from Norway to the people of London was about to be erected.

The London schoolchildren were making their annual pilgrimage to the Central Hall, Westminster, to participate in their carol festival. Across the water, the council meeting ended, with the council going into recess, enabling members to be present at the concert.

It had been raining, with the Thames looking like a shining silver scarf, lights glinting in the water. Trembling on the branches of plane trees, leafless now, raindrops fell like pearls to the glistening pavement. Pigeons and starlings jostled one another energetically, steering for their nightly perches, unheeded by homeward-bound, scurrying crowds. Traffic roared round Parliament Square like the loom of time. The west still held a gleam of gold-fringed cloudscape, the sunset of a winter evening. Was it also the dying twilight of an era?

The great war-time Prime Minister (soon to become Sir Winston), was already sounding his new clarion call "Set the people free". The future rested in the hands of history.

On 2nd June, 1953, in our Hampstead home, my husband and I had been enlivened by the company of two enthusiastic teenagers, my niece and nephew, who had joined us for the great Coronation Day of Queen Elizabeth the Second. We had watched the Abbey service on television and were about to make our way to Hyde Park to see the splendid procession.

Half the tempestuous twentieth century had now flown. There had been a general election in February 1950 which had left Mr. Attlee with a very small majority. Party strife had been overtaken that summer by the outbreak of the Korean war. In September 1951 another parliamentary election had taken place. Mr. Churchill, now aged 77, had found himself once again at the head of the country's affairs in 10 Downing Street.

Rationing had eased. Clothing, footwear, bread, potatoes, jam, sweets, sugar, tea, milk and soap had been freed. In a few months, butter, fats, bacon and meat were to be released.

The theatre was flourishing, together with foreign films and "Espresso" coffee bars. Supermarkets were just beginning. In the cinema the wide-screen technique was rapidly developing. Youth was coming into its own with rock music and jiving, although the era of "The Beatles" and the mini-skirt had yet to dawn.

Looking at the two young people standing beside us, my niece balanced on my husband's shooting stick, I realised that they would soon be clamouring to make their own fashions.

In mid-century Britain, perhaps as never before, Noël Coward's words were ringing true. "It's the younger generation, knock, knock, knocking at the door!"